W9-CPF-755

37635

DATE			

Systems
of
Discourse

Recent Titles in Contributions in Sociology
Series Editor: Don Martindale

Systems
of
Discourse

Structures and Semiotics in the Social Sciences

George V. Zito

Contributions in Sociology, Number 51

Greenwood Press
Westport, Connecticut
London, England

Library of Congress Cataloging in Publication Data

Zito, George V.
  Systems of discourse.

  (Contributions in sociology, ISSN 0084-9278 ; no. 51)
  Bibliography: p.
  Includes index.
  1. Social sciences—Language. 2. Semiotics. I. Title.
II. Series.
H61.Z57 1984   300'.141   83-26668
ISBN 0-313-24446-4 (lib. bdg.)

Library of Congress Catalog Card Number: 83-26668
ISBN: 0-313-24446-4
ISSN: 0084-9278

First published in 1984

Greenwood Press
A division of Congressional Information Service, Inc.
88 Post Road West
Westport, Connecticut 06881

Printed in the United States of America

10 9 8 7 6 5 4 3 2 1

For my daughters, Darlene, Thea, and Pam;
for Ben's daughter, Dorothea;
and for my son, Robin.

Explanation consists merely in analyzing our
complicated systems into simpler systems in
such a way that we recognize, in the complicated
system, the interplay of elements already so familiar
to us that we accept them as not needing explanation.
P. Bridgman, *The Nature of Physical Theory*

An Ultimate Resolution—if one is possible—of
the problem of the intelligibility of the sensible
world must be reserved for some metascience . . . and
it will depend to a great extent on the resolution
of other problems, such as the classical "problem of
causality" and "problem of induction."
E. Nagel, *The Structure of Science*

Contents

Figures and Tables

Figures

Tables

Acknowledgments

This book had its origins in two separate careers, and it is difficult to acknowledge the many persons who contributed to its creation. The most significant contributors from the career to which the book is addressed, sociology, include: Ephraim H. Mizruchi, who beside offering constant encouragement and intellectual stimulation knew when not to ask certain questions, the mark of a true friend. I am indebted to Barry Glassner, who insisted that I write the book in the first place, at a time when I was busy trying to do other things; to Nicholas CH. Tatsis, from our graduate student days until today a fine sounding board for ideas; to Isidor Wallimann, who falls into the same category; and to so many others who in diverse ways contributed an idea here, a thought there. Marnia Lazreg influenced my thinking on these matters when we were both Assistant Professors at the Graduate Faculty of the New School, and the late Emil Oestereicher did so as well. Don Zewe of LeMoyne College was always a patient listener as I droned on in speech, trying to clarify some theoretical point and often found myself lapsing into silence as thoughts came faster than words. And, of course, there were always students, defenseless and forced to hear me out, a captive audience.

In my earlier career, where I invented and built "real" systems and where I underwent more intellectual development than I can ever convey to a reader, there were William R. Polye, my true mentor in engineering physics; Edward Chilton, who shared with me a major portion of my first career; and the late André Viret. The latter two constantly challenged my thinking and made me develop in many different ways, leading me into areas I would otherwise have skirted. It had seemed to me, until now, that I had led two different lives. With this book the continuity becomes clear, and I am pleased to discover that it was one life after all.

Syracuse, New York

Systems
of
Discourse

Language and Social Science: The Historical Background 1

The possibility of a science of signs, a *semiotic*, became evident in both Europe and the United States early in the twentieth century, largely through the efforts of Rudolf Carnap of the Vienna Circle and social behaviorist Charles W. Morris, the student of George Herbert Mead. Such a science of signs necessarily treats language, the sign system par excellence, and early efforts involved specifying the relationships between empirical proofs and their corresponding specification in language. As a result of this effort, a positive formal logic was developed and a movement for the unification of the sciences undertaken. Logical positivism was established and led to the achievements in philosophy of Bertrand Russell and Ludwig Wittgenstein.

At about the same time, Swiss linguist Ferdinand de Saussure was lecturing in Geneva, employing a semiotic very much at odds with that of the logical positivists. He attracted little attention at the time, and what notice was given usually involved the "unscientific" aspect of his model. Like the logical positivists, however, he was quite convinced that there was a relationship between language structures and our understanding of the world. But he saw that language was a social product and that as such it suffered many of the vagaries and imprecisions of all such social "things." Since it was essentially social, it should find its greatest application in the social sciences instead of in the natural sciences that interested the logical positivists.

Saussure realized that "by studying rites, customs, etc., as signs," one could explain them by "the laws of semiotics." He was eager to point out that such linguistic semiotics "must be set apart from anthropology, which studies man solely from the viewpoint of his species, for language is a social fact. But must it then be combined with sociology? What are the relationships between linguistics and social psychology?"

Saussure's question remained unnoticed until the twentieth century was half over, and it did not attain notoriety in the social sciences until the closing quarter. True, semiotics could deal with signs, and language was a system of signs. Also, language could be shown to perform significant symbolic functions in human interactions, functions of significance not only to sociologists and social psychologists but also to psychologists generally. But aside from attempts to join social psychology to logical positivism, and experiments to study verbal interactions in small laboratory groups, linguistic models seemed unproductive. When halfway through the twentieth century French anthropologist Claude Lévi-Strauss began applying a method of analysis to primitive peoples predicated on a linguistic semiotic model, his pioneeering efforts went virtually unnoticed. This indifference was due not only to the semiotic nature of the method but also to the state of the social sciences.

The appropriate method of investigation has always been the subject of considerable debate in the social sciences. A controversy exists with respect to the applicability of models or paradigms, the extent to which causal relations of a social kind are related to those causal relations considered by the natural sciences, the emphasis to be placed on structures rather than on cultural influences, and the relative significance of subjectivist, phenomenologically oriented investigations in the specification of collective properties of organization and activity. None of these is a trivial matter for social scientists, who are still wrestling with differences between the positivist and humanist traditions.

It was into this theoretical and methodological morass that Lévi-Strauss boldly ventured with his *Les structures elementaires de la parenté* in 1949, employing a method for the analysis of kinship predicated on a linguistic semiotic model. The reception was not enthusiastic. It was not until 1969 that Rodney Needham offered an English translation, *The Elementary Structures of Kinship*, and this translation saw publication only through the efforts of the Unitarian-Universalist publishing house, Beacon Press, in Boston, which had limited distribution facilities. With this publication however, French structuralism, the application of a semiotic system of language to everything social, was born. A collection of Lévi-Strauss's papers in anthropology, entitled *Structural Anthropology* and published in France in 1958 and in the United States in 1963, had aroused little interest. In the English-speaking world the time was not yet suitable for one more methodological paradigm.

Developments in analytical philosophy and in phenomenology had been introduced into sociological agendas at the time when a synthesis of earlier social theories by American sociologist Talcott Parsons was well under way and had already approached institutionalization at the university level. A rediscovery of the philosophical Marx, spurred at first by the publication of the *Paris Manuscripts* and later of the *Grundrisse*, caused a flurry of excitement in light of what had been perceived as the postwar "challenge" of existentialism. Novel interpretive approaches, often interesting blends of Marxism, Freudianism, existentialism, and phenomenalism, contended among themselves and with an inherited positivism for domination of the sociological marketplace. When during the 1960s it became apparent that the promised solution was not at hand, the social sciences were left in a state of disarray. Sociologists and their colleagues beat a hurried retreat back to the "classical" founding fathers. New editions and translations of the works of the Durkheimians, of Georg Simmel, Karl Marx, Max Weber, and the Frankfurt school members began to appear. English social scientists rediscovered the Americans, Park and Burgess and reconsidered sociology as a possible alternative to their anthropology. The French, who had never abandoned Durkheim and his *Année* heirs in their flirtations with Marx, discovered French-Swiss linguist Ferdinand de Saussure. Saussure had been a contemporary of Durkheim, and his analysis of symbolic systems, and particularly of language, was seen to complement Durkheim's *Rules of the Sociological Method* in a remarkable way and to supply connections missing in the the the *Année* enterprise. At this point Lévi-Strauss announced the birth of structuralism. As the century draws to a close, the hurried flirtation with structuralism by European intellectuals is already in decline, while in the United States it is only sluggishly under way. It has made few inroads in Britain, where its linguistic orientation is seen to offer little more than what had already been accomplished from a literary standpoint by James Joyce and other writers of what Stephen Spender termed "the Modernist movement" some fifty years earlier. Indeed, it may be that French structuralism, as an intellectual movement, will mirror the earlier history of French symbolism, when an inept translation of the poetry of Edgar Allan Poe introduced into French literature an element of expression it had curiously lacked.[1] Such symbolic representation is the common concern of both movements. French preoccupation with Émile Durkheim's stress on collective representations, particularly as enunciated in his later and perhaps greatest work, *The Elementary Forms of the Religious Life*, and developed further by Maurice Halbwachs, Marcel Mauss, Paul Fauconnet, and others of the *Année* school, is particularly amenable to the kind of treatment semiotics (or semiology) can offer. It is here suggested that French social thought has undergone the same kind of transformation the earlier French literary enterprise underwent, and for many of the same reasons. In particular, Durkheim's contribution provided a ready soil for a previously neglected mode of analysis. One does not expect so welcome a reception for structuralism among English-speaking communities, and there has not been any.

Structuralism has had to confront the same epistemological problems that produced the present impasse in the social sciences: the nature of causality and intentionality, the distinction between social things and things of other kinds, methodological procedures, and the culture versus structure problem. It was able to do so with considerable ease, although the results were not sufficiently utilitarian to warrant its institutionalization at the American or British universities. Its neglect of the empirical dimension, an unpardonable sin to the heirs of pragmatism, made it "speculative," and therefore to be ignored as unscientific. In addition, the idea of a system it employed was so obscure compared to those traditionally employed by the social sciences that it appeared "unsystematic," if not haphazard. Many of the complaints levied against structuralism smack of the same biases as those levied against the work of Georg Simmel a generation earlier. It was also somewhat positivistic and slightly Marxist, an apparent contradiction to many American sociologists.

Nonetheless, French structuralism, as proposed by Lévi-Strauss and as extended by Michel Foucault and others, is systematic and does depend on the notion of a system. Because at this juncture the structuralist response to the problems of theory and method confronting the social sciences differs considerably from what American social scientists expect, it is necessary to grasp the idea of a system implicit in its literature. This idea runs through the work of Claude Lévi-Strauss and penetrates the work of Foucault, whether the latter be considered "structuralist" or "post-structuralist,"[2] or perhaps merely "post-systematic structuralist." In the present book, this idea of a system is explicated and applied to examples drawn from sociological discourses. In performing these operations, it is not my intention either to promote the method or to detract from it, although at times I may appear to be doing one or the other. It is because the idea of a system employed by structuralism merits serious attention, that I have striven to extract this idea. The very fact that it is an idea at odds with other ideas of systems we have met in the social sciences and elsewhere is sufficient reason to explicate it.

In attempting to define this system, we are presented with certain obstacles. First, what has been called "structuralism" is relatively unorganized, with no acknowledged spokesperson. Also, many writers identified by their publics as "structuralist" disdain the label. For example, Foucault concludes his discussion in "The Discourse on Language" with the disclaimer "And now, let those who are weak on vocabulary, let those with little comprehension of theory call all this—if its appeal is stronger than its meaning for them—structuralism."[3] Similarly, Charles Lemert and Willard Nielsen assert, "We are not structuralists, but we are not going to waste space and time with a history of the theoretical materials we use."[4] Part of the problem is that what has been loosely termed "structuralism" has gone through several stages, the most recent stage being less mechanistic and formal than the earlier. Another part of the problem is that the philosophical underpinnings governing the discourse are in many instances derived directly from other sources (Karl Marx, Martin Heidegger, and Leonard Bloomfield) than the Saussurian and *Année* origins governing "French" structuralism. Louis Althusser, Lucien Goldmann, Jacques Derrida—"structuralists" of this "other" sort—join with the latter only in a common concentration on language or discourse. For example, Jacques Laçan is first of all a Freudian and Althusser is first a Marxist. And there is the earlier use of the term "structuralism" in the social sciences which has little or nothing to do with language. Jean Piaget, in his little book *Structuralism*, includes theorists like Kurt Lewin and Talcott Parsons in his discussion, neither of whom would be included in either of the above categories. To the extent that they share a common concern with language, Parsons, along with Theodore Mills, Robert F. Bales, Fred Strodtbeck, and Edward Shils, clearly descends from a quite different tradition, one treating signs in positivist terms according to a model very different from that proposed by de Saussure. Parsons has commented on differences between his own approach and that of Lévi-Strauss, and his comments appear to hold for all the so-called Harvard school of sociology.[5]

To circumvent these difficulties, the discussion in the following chapters is limited by defining as "structuralist" only efforts that claim to derive some of their methods or theoretical bases from the series of lectures on semiotics delivered by Ferdinand Saussure at Geneva in 1907–1911 and subsequently compiled and published in 1916 by Charles Bally and Albert Sechehaye as *Cours de linguistique generale*. In English-language editions, the *Course in General Linguistics* has been available since 1959.[6] The idea of a system will be extracted from the Saussure book. In addition, the discussion will be limited largely to some works of Lévi-Strauss, the "father of French structuralism" in the social sciences, and to some of the work of Michel Foucault. Foucault's work represents the furthest development of Saussure's idea of a system, although he finally goes beyond it.[7] We will not consider his nonstructuralist efforts. This concentration on the system and its implications for the philosophy of science necessarily excludes not only those theorists whose work is tangential to Saussure's thrust but also those who (like Lucien Goldmann, Jacques Laçan, Louis Althusser, Jean Piaget, and others) are drawn less to this systematic feature than to literary or Marxist concerns.[8] This idea of a system is most useful in explicating the various problematic assumptions determining the ideas of causality, essence, and meaning—all concerns of any philosophy of social science. The relevant ideas touching on these matters will be extracted, since these are of some concern to the social sciences, particularly in light of the claim that French structuralism derives as much from Durkheim as from Saussure.[9]

That a complex set of relationships exists between language and society is certainly not news for the social scientist. As the structuralist literature indicates, however, this is not simply the consequence of language being a social product; in many respects, society may be a product of language. Both language and society are things we are born into, and both constrain our ability to conceptualize and perhaps make thinking itself possible. We can conceive of a human society based wholly on oral traditions, lacking a written language or system of signs, but we cannot conceive of a human society where speech is wholly

absent. Speech is an elemental social phenomenon, involving ex-
changes of the most necessary and immediate kind. The system of language, and of languages, merits the closest attention we are capable of
providing. For structuralists, this system becomes the paragon of all
other systems.[10] From this perspective, what we have usually called
"the social system" requires extensive revision.

At the level of conscious awareness, the average native speaker of
a language does not know the rules governing the language he speaks.
His language seems natural, automatic, innate, much as the existence
of the world seems natural. For this reason the native speaker is often
perplexed and sometimes confusedly amused by the efforts of grammarians, lexicographers, and linguists to explain to him the rules of
syntax and grammar governing his language. Similarly, he is apt to be
cynical and sometimes contemptuous of social scientists' efforts to explain the norms, roles, status allocations, and values of the society he
finds himself born into. He feels (and perhaps quite rightly) that such
rules of grammar and syntax, and such notions as norms, roles, and
the like, are mere ideas, formulated by academics *after* the facts of
language and society and not prior to them. Such hypothetical rules
are accordingly not binding and have no tangible existence in the "real
world" he inhabits. They are merely the consequences, expressed in
esoteric nomenclatures, of quite ordinary people speaking and living.
Their so-called "rules" are only inferences that cannot be proven to
be so, made by people with certain kinds of education, people involved in a reality of their own, at odds with the real world. He feels
that these people have not been authorized to speak for him, and that
they cannot rightfully demand that people listen to them. They may
claim what they call "institutional authority," but this is an abstraction without legal force. At any rate, the real existence of such "institutions" is doubtful. The ordinary person sees that people who continually speak about institutions do so in class-specific ways rather than
in the manner of the natural sciences. For such a person, perhaps only
the natural sciences are indeed sciences; the mention of a social science is apt to bring a smile.

We cannot claim that this average native speaker of a language is
wrong and that we are right. Indeed, the structuralist effort shows that
the reverse is probably true: we in the social sciences tend to become
trapped by the structures of our own discourse in ways that the average

speaker does not. Our discourse necessarily distances us from the spontaneity of language and the quixotic events of social life. The ordinary person, the person who employs language only for its appropriate function (to communicate to another social being "what's on his mind" in the hope that the other person will understand what he intends), seldom finds it necessary to reflect on language or society. Indeed, an excess of such reflection may inhibit or confuse speech and interaction by overly constraining its otherwise free and apparently natural flow. A tongue-tied Hamlet, unable to speak or to act, is a consummation devoutly to be avoided.

Yet it is clear that language and the world are not naturally given, but must be acquired by the individual. What is glossed over in psychology and sociology texts as *socialization* and *interaction* is at work here, although we do not really understand the processes involved. George Herbert Mead, John Dewey, Alfred North Whitehead, and hosts of educators and social psychologists have worried over this theoretical difficulty without resolving it. To the layman, explanations of these phenomena often appear to have the general characteristics of other fads and fashions: they follow cycles of popularity with little retention of previous materials. There is some general agreement that socialization is never wholly complete and that the individual mind is finally unsuccessful in its attempts to comprehend fully the external constraints imposed on it by a world it has inherited rather than created. This view was developed by Georg Simmel early in the twentieth century: the individual can never be wholly within the society he inhabits without simultaneously being outside it; a dialectical contradiction exists in the very existence of life as the primary moving force of the social world. But other theorists were eager to translate this contradiction into positivistic metaphors and thereby generate a pathology of the social world. Sigmund Freud postulated a clearly demarked division within consciousness, only one segment of which, the superego, was of social origin. He contended that there was a "natural" component of mind which was antagonistic to the external constraints of social existence. For Freud and his disciples, advances in civilization—the increased sophistication of worldly constructions or the development of spirit in its Hegelian sense—could only estrange the individual from his ontologically "natural" component. This naturalistic emphasis on the "real" or "true" nature of the human individual implied the amenability of the methods of the natural sciences for its exploration, delineation, and

control, and a therapy to correct what were perceived as merely pro-
gramming errors.

The positivistic emphasis of Freudianism involved a grounding of
the human mind in the natural order, but at the same time it deem-
phasized the Cartesian mind-matter dichotomy. The outcome of this
new emphasis can be seen in the separate concerns of both scientific
and popular cultures. On the one hand, there are the advances in neu-
robiology that within this particular mode of discourse help explain the
binary oppositions implicit in the neuronic structures which (it is now
believed) explain the process of thinking which gives rise to mind. On
the other hand, there is within popular culture a search on the part of
individuals for some intrinsic, nonsocial personal ''self'' believed to
be natural and quite apart from the externally imposed and hence ''in-
valid'' claims of inherited cultural contexts. It is important to note that
in both cases, what has shifted is the grounding of the world itself—
from a grounding in mind to a grounding in the physical, in matter.

This grounding of the world in physiology has in turn led to certain
changes in perspectives within the social sciences. There is the novel
insistence on the transmission of culture among subhuman species
(monkeys on Japanese islands, birds without beaks in forests abound-
ing in borers, and efforts, fortunately unsuccessful, to teach porpoises
to speak and apes to operate computers). From quite another direction,
there is increased emphasis on discovering what things ''really are'' in
the state of being themselves, new varieties of phenomenalism holding
that, since mind is physiologically based, new reductions of an order
quite different from the Cartesian are required to unmask an essential
reality from the meanings we have imposed on it. Implicit in all such
efforts is a monistic bias that some kind of congruency is possible between things-in-themselves and the capacity of the knowing mind.

The grounding of the world in physiology has also led to certain
other developments, such as those we consider in the following chapters. Structuralism offers the possibility that much, if not all, of both
language and society is physiologically based. At the same time, it avoids
the teleological assumptions implied in the idea of phenomenological
essence and in the notions of manifest and latent functions of structural
functionalism. It is peculiarly at odds with competing efforts in the social sciences that stress Edmund Husserl's concept of intentionality,
although intentionality plays an important part in it. In the essays that
follow, we attempt to sort out the often conflicting tendencies within

what is here termed "contemporary structuralism." It may be that structuralism will suffer the same fate as other intellectual movements of the twentieth century—symbolism, existentialism, systems theory, and the like—which for all their promise seem to have contributed little in the final analysis. But like these movements, structuralism can be expected to leave certain residues in our language which, on its own premises, will continue to affect the ways in which we speak about the world and how we relate to other persons and things within it.

Notes

1. For an early but still authoritative discussion of the connection between French symbolism and the work of Edgar Allan Poe, see Edmund Wilson, *Axel's Castle: A Study of the Imaginative Literature of 1870–1930* (New York: Scribner's, 1931).

2. Foucault's work presents something of a problem. Ino Rossi (in *Structural Sociology*, ed. Ino Rossi [New York: Columbia University Press, 1982], p. 3) says, "The systematic phase of semiotics has dealt with the syntactic structure of semiotic systems rather than with the social processes producing the syntactic structure or with the social usage of language. The latter focus of analysis has characterized the works of postsystematic semioticians, prominent among whom are the literary critics Julia Kristeva and the more recent works of Roland Barthes. Michel Foucault, a philosopher often labelled as 'structuralist,' also has focused on discursive formations as a strategy indispensable to understanding particular texts," and cites Charles C. Lemert's *Sociology and the Twilight of Man* (Carbondale: Southern Illinois University Press, 1979) as his reference for the statement. In Rossi's *Structural Sociology*, p. 329, Lemert and co-author Willard A. Nielsen assert, "We believe that the distinctive features of structuralism truly emerge only in the later movement, post-structuralism, which made explicit the critiques of historicism, subject reductionism, metaphysics and—generally—homocentric humanism. Post-structuralism's *loci classici* are Foucault's *Archaeologie de savoir* or Derrida's *De la grammatologie*, while structuralism's point of reference is Lévi-Strauss's *Les structures elementaires de la parenté*. In both lines, discourse (mythic, poetic, vocal, etc.) is the primary surface of investigation, but it is only in the former cases that the embeddedness of language and discursive practices in concrete social formulations is taken as essential." If the distinctive features of structuralism do emerge in "post-structuralism," then the latter cannot be excluded from the category "structuralism"; that is, "post-structuralism" is an element of the set "structuralism." Foucault is accordingly included within the structuralist camp, as are Lemert and Nielsen, within our understanding of

the term. In the context of the present book, "postsystematic" (as employed by Rossi) is confounding and is not employed.

3. Michel Foucault, "The Discourse on Language," in his *Archaeology of Knowledge* (New York: Harper & Row, 1976). This "discourse" is important for an understanding of Foucault's work. "It is sometimes supposed that Foucault's subsequent thematisation of power tacitly jettisons as obsolete the ambitious methodological edifice of the *Archaelogy*. In fact the features of the latter . . . form the essential ground for the further concepts Foucault was to introduce. . . . First, in his 1970 lecture, 'The Order of Discourse,' Foucault shows how the rules of formation of discourses are linked to the operation of a particular kind of social power. Discourses not only exhibit immanent principles of regularity, they are also bound by regulations enforced through social practises of appropriation, control and policing. Discourse is a polemical commodity" (Colin Gordon, "Afterword," in Michel Foucault's *Power/Knowledge* [New York: Pantheon, 1980], p. 245). The lecture Gordon refers to is "L'ordre du discours," translated by Rupert Swyer as "The Discourse on Language" and cited at the beginning of this note.

4. Charles C. Lemert and Willard A. Nielsen, Jr., "Structures, Instruments, and Reading in Sociology," in Rossi, 1982, p. 351.

5. Talcott Parsons, "Action, Symbols, and Cybernetic Control," in Rossi, 1982, p. 49ff.

6. Saussure's *Course in General Linguistics* was first published in English by the Philosophical Library in 1959; it was reprinted in a paperback edition by McGraw-Hill Book Co. in 1966.

7. What we are doing, therefore, is explicating the idea of a system in structuralist thought, instead of providing a critique of all the works of Lévi-Strauss or Foucault. If the latter were attempted, we would have to consider many other books, lectures, and interviews. There are works by both authors that are clearly not structuralist.

8. Introductory readings on structuralism include Jonathan Culler's *Ferdinand de Saussure* (Baltimore: Penguin, 1976) and *Structuralist Poetics* (Ithaca, N.Y.: Cornell University Press, 1975); Jean Piaget's *Structuralism* (New York: Harper & Row, 1968); this must be read cautiously, however, as already suggested; Jacques Ehrmann's *Structuralism* (Garden City, N.Y.: Doubleday, 1966) is a good edited set of readings; Philip Pettit's *The Concept of Structuralism* (Berkeley: University of California Press, 1977), generally misreads Saussure in favor of Noam Chomsky but includes good bibliographic materials; and Terrence Hawkins's *Structuralism and Semiotics* (Berkeley: University of California Press, 1977), which is concerned less with social science than with literature but reads quickly and is well done.

9. In this connection, see Simon Clarke's "The Origins of Lévi-Strauss's Structuralism," *Sociology* 12(3), 1978; C. R. Badcock's "The Ecumenical Anthropologist: Solutions to Some Persistent Problems in Theoretical Sociol-

ogy Found in the Works of Claude Lévi-Strauss,'' *British Journal of Sociology* 26(2), 1975; Zygmunt Bauman's ''The Structuralist Promise,'' *British Journal of Sociology* 24(1), 1973.

10. This is shown by the efforts of Umberto Eco to revive the Carnap-Morris positivistic semiotic in his *A Theory of Semiotics* (Bloomington: Indiana University Press, 1976). Clearly anti-Saussurian, Eco employs methods that are nonstructuralist and is highly critical of Lévi-Strauss. He mentions Foucault only once: ''But what Foucault (1966) has written on the 'epistemes' of different epochs and the variations in their segmentation of the universe, or what Lévi-Strauss (1962) has written on the taxonomy of primitive people, should suffice to make us aware that even on these points it is wise to proceed with caution'' (p. 79). After a long discussion of the ''fallacy in Lévi-Strauss's discussion on the 'linguistic' properties of paintings'' (p. 228), Eco concludes that his considerations ''force one to recognize that it is wrong to believe . . . that every sign system act is based on a 'language' similar to the verbal one'' (p. 231), thus rejecting a principal tenet of what is referred to as contemporary structuralism.

Systems of Action 2

Karl Mannheim reminds us that the search for origins involves the seeker in an infinite regression.[1] Precursors may always be found for some idea or approach to understanding, and once they have been uncovered they lead to other earlier sources. With respect to current usage of the idea of a system, Mannheim's observation is particularly acute. The definition of the word "system" given in the *Oxford English Dictionary* occupies more than a full page, exceeding three columns of fine print. Proceeding from there to the Greek lexicon is ultimately unrewarding. From the earliest records, the idea of an organized whole appears fully developed. At the present time this idea is not limited to holism in its various philosophical forms[2] but is applied to a wide variety of phenomena of more limited kinds—some concrete, others quite abstract and speculative. There seems to be some agreement, however, that what we mean by a system is no mere aggregate of parts but a whole composed of interdependent units or elements. It is not always clear whether this interdependence is organized according to some intrinsic property of the elements themselves or whether the organizing principle is imposed on it solely for purposes of analysis. This is important in the designation of systems involving some form of activity or action.

We can set aside consideration of systems that are merely classificatory, characterized by typological organization alone, and limit the discussion to systems of action, since these are of particular significance in social-scientific explanation.

A conventional mousetrap is an action system under this definition. Its spring loads the snare, which is held in place by a rod latched to the bait lure. Each element of the system (spring, snare, latch, and lure) performs only one discrete operation in the overall system. We refer to such operations as *functions*. Thus, the function of the latch is to restrain the effort of the spring while the system is in a quiescent state, waiting to perform its activity; conversely, the function of the latch is to release the energy of the spring when the system is called on to perform its overall function. Both systems and the elements comprising them have functions. Such functions may be defined in a variety of ways, but the definitions must always encode the operation performed in terms of the element and something in addition to it, such as a contingent element, an operating state, or an activity of some kind.

It is clear that such a system cannot function in the absence of an environment (that is, someone must load the trap and set it, this must be done somewhere, and a mouse is required to enable the system to function properly). It is also clear that many such systems can be simultaneously placed within the same environment.

In this case, what is termed *interdependency* is organized according to intrinsic properties of the elements themselves; the latch cannot perform the function of the spring, and the bait lure cannot perform the function of the snare. The *form* as well as the function of each element is determined by its relation to every other element and the part it plays in the overall operation of the system. The elements are therefore *not* interchangeable, nor are their functions. Moreover, the mousetrap involves one in a rather blatant teleology: it cannot have organized itself and come into being independent of some intentionality external to itself. It has definable limits, and it exhibits no morphogenetic features. There is an underlying intention and purposiveness in its fixed design.

A judicial system, like the mousetrap, is an action system, involving purposiveness and intentionality. It too exists in some environment, but it differs in its origins, elements, and functions. It is not the product of a single mind, as was the mousetrap, and probably did not emerge as a fully developed system but required both time and the effort of many to bring it to its most recent form. It is unclear whether a judicial system contains morphogenetic features, or redundant elements, and its outermost limits are difficult to define. Its elements, such as we can determine by process of analysis, may also be described and understood in terms of the functions they perform in the operation of the system as a whole. The judicial system also operates in some environment and requires some exogenous agent like the mouse to set it into operation.

It is clear that a mode of analysis may be developed that treats judicial systems and mousetraps according to their constituitive elements and the functions performed by these elements in the operation of the system as a whole.

These systems may themselves be parts of larger systems and serve functions in those systems of which they are subsystems, but this need not concern us in our attempts to analyze and understand them as systems in their own right. Insofar as they perform some overall functional operation resulting in action, we may treat their endogenous components as elements of the environment to which they connect. If we insist that we must understand the total environment of the mousetrap and the judicial system prior to any attempt on our part to analyze them, then we once again begin that process of infinite regression and are called on to understand the entire universe before we are able to understand anything in it. This variety of holism is clearly untenable.[3] What is useful, opportune, and functionally necessary for understanding involves boundaries specifiable in terms of the immediate phenomenon itself. Knowledge of the hydrogen cycle in the Orion Horsehead nebula, although it constitutes a component of the environment of my cellar mousetrap, need not be taken into account as an exogenous variable in my analysis of the operation of the mousetrap as a system. For the purposes of my understanding, phenomena demonstrably remote according to the rules of my understanding may be neglected. While such a position carries the risk of error, it enables me to undertake a process of evaluation which is otherwise closed to me. In short, any analytical process must begin with some definable phenomenon less than totality itself and progress by inductive and deductive procedures seeking to specify relationships among elements. It 'seems reasonable' then, that I may analyze the functions, elements, and operations of the mousetrap system (or of any system) according to its own properties and concern myself with the specific portion of the environment which interfaces with the system only in some necessary and functional way; for example, the appetite of mice and the applied force of their jaws are necessary concerns, for they are involved directly as elements of the environment in setting the mousetrap system in operation in a way that the Horsehead nebula is not.

The mousetrap is not an interactive or adaptive system. An *interactive* system involves some measure of reciprocity with its environment. The mousetrap, once triggered, simply goes through a series of steps, and once actions have been completed, it ceases to function until reset by some environmental factor. An interactive system is able to modify its performance continuously in response to variations in its environment. A toy kite, with its tail and string, constitutes such an interactive system. It adapts to changes in wind velocity and direction by shifting its position to maintain its flight; the tail helps steer it into the wind's direction, and the anchoring string enables it either to climb or to maintain its position. Kite, tail, string, and anchor comprise a system of elements, and the system so constituted is able to tolerate a wide variation of environmental factors by translating them into its own functional requirements. The kite system clearly adapts to and interacts with its environment in a way that the mousetrap does not.

The application of general systems theory to social science considers its objects of inquiry in terms of such adaptive systems in which interactive processes take place.[4] Earlier mechanistic analysis of social systems tended to employ mousetrap models in which elements are considered as variables that are linear functions similar to bait, spring, latch, and bar. A quantitative path analysis, for example, is based upon a mousetrap model of society. Some exogenous variable plays the part of the mouse, while endogenous variables are so arranged that each is a linear device (such as lure, bait, bar) that is set into sequential operation toward some dependent desideratum such as *social mobility*, *level of status attainment*, or *divorce rate*. They are recursive models that, systems theorists would hold, bear little resemblance to the world of social reality. That world appears to be characterized by interactive processes where effects modify or influence causes in nonrecursive ways, where my response to you is modified by my awareness of your expectations of me, which are in turn modified by your understanding of my understanding of such expectations. Recursive models of interactional systems cannot deal with such systems, where "effects" modify their "causes" in this way.

Any adaptive or interactive system functions because it is able to sense changes in its environment and make the necessary corrections to maintain its functional status within specifiable limits or tolerances. It thus performs a variety of system maintenance, but only in the sense that it can maintain its operation within design limits. It is important to specify clearly that "maintenance" here implies only an ability to continue to operate by adapting to strains consistent with the properties of elements—the strength of its string, the weight of its tail, and so forth, in the case of the kite—and the strains imposed on it by its environment which it is able to translate, by way of its elemental functions, into its systemic operation. It contains no component or subsystem specific to this maintenance task. A wind too strong will rip the kite apart or break the string, in which case the systemic operation ceases. The operation of system maintenance here does not imply morphogenetic properties: the kite cannot itself generate new features enabling it to withstand stronger winds or to fly higher. It cannot patch its own torn skin. Thus, while system maintenance is a property of any adaptive system, self-healing, or morphogenesis, is not a necessary property of a system by virtue of that system's being adaptive.

Although certain systems, such as biological systems, may include both self-healing and morphogenetic properties, they do not do so by virtue of their being adaptive systems. Neither do they do so as a consequence of any nonrecursive processes in and of themselves. These are additional features that may function to improve the adaptability of a system to its environment and hence enable it to operate satisfactorily (within its functional imperatives) over wider limits or tolerances within its environment. However, no system we know of is altogether immune to its environmental strains: sails rip and masts break, human beings experience heart attacks and strokes, hoisting cranes buckle and airplanes crash in ice storms.

The application of systems theory to social phenomena need not be predicated on a biological analogue, as the adaptive system model does not require self-healing and morphogenesis. All that is required is a set of interrelated elements functioning so as to maintain the system's operation interactively with certain environments.

Mousetraps and kites are designed as systems, with their functional elements constructed to optimize system performance. In the case of biological or social systems, however, the very idea of a system may only be inferred, independent of any intentional design. Biological, social, language, and systems of numerous other kinds are systems only to the extent that we are able to understand them in terms of the interrelationships among their constituitive elements and to the extent that we can define them as elements. They are systems we are born into which exist prior to our understanding of them in systemic terms. Their very existence *as* systems is therefore a consequence of our analysis of them and our willingness to treat them according to principles discovered not in themselves but in systems of our intentional creation.

When applied to animals and societies, the idea of a system is clearly an heuristic analytical device. It is useful in its ability to specify possible relations among different kinds of activity, and it assists us in our clarification of the part that may be played in social processes by the patterns of organization which have been passed on to us. Systems theory proposes a method of analysis, treating complex phenomena in terms of their interrelated functioning elements in an attempt to discover if anything new can be learned about these phenomena. It makes no exclusive claim to the reality of the phenomena. It translates its objects of concern into its own formulas and nomenclature in an effort to demonstrate certain cross-systems similarities and differences. The similarities and differences are not necessarily dictated by its own mode of analysis, however, although it may find it convenient to designate them in its own nomenclature. For example, the difference between a kite system and a mousetrap system, in terms of their functions, is neither arbitrary nor a difference that results from our treatment of them as systems.

It is because of the ability to treat many complex wholes in terms of relatively few basic principles that systems theory appears to have so much to offer the social sciences, although its promise has been largely unfulfilled. Neuromuscular systems, electronic guidance and control, planetary and interplanetary systems, collectivities that are not mere aggregates but interdependent parts somehow operating together (such as societies and smaller groups)—are all amenable to systems theory analysis. Since it is the interrelatedness of functioning parts that is the locus of concern, mathematical techniques may often be applied in the analysis which allow us to understand a dynamic rather than a static state of operation. Thus it appears possible to rise above the mousetrap level of explanation of conventional social-scientific methodologies and employ a calculus of change capable of dealing with the nonlinear aspects of what we take to comprise social reality.

If, as has been suggested, the social is characterized by interactive processes of a nonrecursive nature (as Simmel, Mauss, Mead, and others have suggested), then it would appear that systems analysis would be well suited to their study since it is able to specify this in terms of feedback processes. Since feedback appears to be present in all nonrecursive systems, its emergence and treatment in systems theory gives it particular importance.

It became evident during World War II that fairly simple guidance and control systems could be built for vehicles that utilized a feedback principle. What is today designated as "systems theory" is a direct development of principles and mathematical expressions of this technological origin, particularly in the area of servomechanisms.[5] Servomechanisms were themselves refinements of an earlier technology in hydraulics employed to stabilize oceangoing vessels.

A simple Boy Scout pocket compass is a variety of a mousetrap system. A magnetized needle is balanced on a pivot and placed above a calibrated card. The magnetized needle aligns itself with the earth's magnetic field in its environment. If the boy scout rotates the calibrated card so that the shiny part of the needle lies above the designation N, all other points of the compass are immediately specified. If the boy scout wishes to travel east, he moves in the direction of E on the card; periodically, he must reconsider the compass, correcting his travel from time to time, since he may unwittingly deviate from the East heading, or because of local variations in the terrain and magnetic variations.[6]

We may place some coils of wire around such a compass. A moving magnetized vane, such as a compass needle, will cause an electrical current to flow in a coil of wire. The same principle is employed in generating commercial electrical power. In the case of the compass, we can arrange the coils and magnetized needle so that the greater the deviation from North, the greater the strength of the current that is produced. Moreover, we can so arrange them that deviations from North in an easterly direction will produce a signal that is positive in polarity, while deviations from the north in a westerly direction will produce a signal that is negative, though retaining the feature that *the greater the deviation, the stronger the signal.*

Employing such a device as one element of a system, we can be sure that an aircraft (or any vehicle) will automatically steer itself to the north—or, with minor modification in the form of a bias signal, steer itself in any direction we choose. This is the principle employed in automatic pilots and similar guidance and control systems used in commercial airliners. Figure 2.1 shows such a simple, compass-guided system. The electrical signals produced by the compass are amplified

Figure 2.1
An Aircraft Automatic Pilot

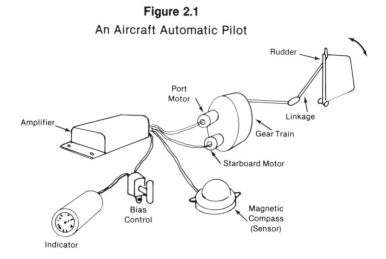

to a level high enough to enable them to operate motors to actuate the steering rudder. The pictorial representation in Figure 2.1, however, makes it difficult to visualize how the system operates. The figure shows us only the shape of components employed in the system and tells us nothing about their functions as systemic elements; the assortment of parts could be any kind of aggregate and not a true system at all. Therefore a system of schematic representation is used to present the elements as a series of black boxes, where the interconnections and functions of the elements of the system may be clearly shown.

Such a functional, schematic presentation of the components shown in Figure 2.1 is given in Figure 2.2. This representation tells us much more than the pictorial representation and allows for analysis of the system. Each element is represented here as a box, so that its functional nature, rather than its physical appearance in a particular embodiment of the system, becomes the focus of attention. In conjunction with each box, the transfer function of each element is specified in quantitative electrical or other physical units. Hence, in looking at the black box representation, we can see that should the vehicle con-

Figure 2.2

Schematic Representation of the
Automatic Pilot Shown in Figure 2.1

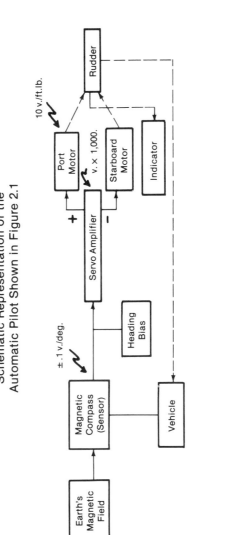

trolled by the system deviate from North by 5 degrees in heading, the sensor will produce about half of 1 volt (since its transfer function is specified as .1 volt per degree). The polarity of this voltage will be determined by whether this 5-degree deviation is toward East or toward West. In either case, this .5 volt signal will be amplified by a factor of 1,000 by the amplifier, providing 500 volts at the output of the amplifier to power the motors. Since the motors and gear train have the capability (their transfer function) of exerting 1 foot pound of force for each 10 volts applied to them, then 50 foot pounds will be applied to the rudder in that direction to steer the vessel toward the north. The output of the sensor is the input of the amplifier, and the output of the amplifier is the input to the motors. "Input" and "output" are terms that apply to each of the black boxes according to the direction of signal flow or, in Talcott Parsons's terms, "the direction of cybernetic control." A transfer function specifies the relation of the output to the input and is all we need to know of the properties of any black box to include it within the analysis of the system. Its appearance, size, weight, and so on are irrelevant properties from the standpoint of system-functioning.

The critical consideration of all such interactive systems is its non-recursive operation. As soon as the above force is applied to the rudder and it begins moving in the direction specified by the signal, the vehicle begins to move accordingly. But this means that the signal now being generated by the sensor decreases in magnitude to something less than .5 volts and that the motors accordingly deflect the rudder by a smaller displacement. This process continues, with the sensor continually furnishing to the rest of the system the decreasing deviation it is sensing from the desired North heading. The effect of this is present throughout the system. The "cause" of this "effect" is being continually changed or modified by the "effect" itself. There is no step-by-step operation, as in the mousetrap, but a continuous proportional activity constantly changing as the objective of the system is approached.

If the vehicle was initially heading west, as shown in Figure 2.3, the action of the system is not such that the vehicle follows the course indicated by the dashed line; this would be the case only if the system was not constantly measuring its present performance in terms of its goal. Since the information passing through the system in the form of a signal combines both cause and effect into one, and the motors are only responding to this information, the vehicle approaches the desired heading as shown in Figure 2.3b. It approaches the line of the course asymptotically and is finally aligned with it.

In real situations, the inertia of the vehicle is sufficiently high to preclude the smooth asymptote shown in Figure 2.3b. A well-designed servo control system guides the vehicle into alignment as shown in Figure 2.3c, allowing perhaps one small "overshoot" and then "locking on." A poorly designed or defective system may result in one of two alternatives: the system may continuously overshoot, hunting back and forth as in Figure 2.3d, or it may suffer complete loss of control and oscillate wildly, as in Figure 2.3f. These control conditions may all be represented by sets of differential equations[7] and the system designed taking these into account. Similarly, the system may be analyzed for stability by employing these equations. Conditions of instability are most often the result of too much or too little feedback. By studying the set of transfer functions and the amount of feedback, the overall performance of the system can be predicted.

The preceding did not specify the feedback path, but we can see it

Figure 2.3
Automatic Pilot Performance

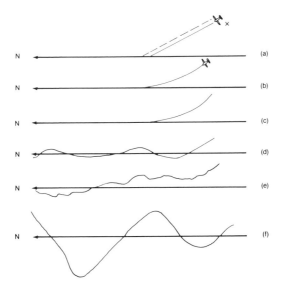

clearly in Figure 2.2. The sensor determines the movement of the rudder, which determines the attitude of the vehicle, which determines the sensor's relationship to the earth's magnetic field, which determines the sensor's output, which determines the movement of the rudder, and so on. This is a nonrecursive, adaptive system, where *cause* and *effect* simultaneously modify each other. A closed loop exists, linking the functions of the elements in a continuously circulating overall process. A measurement made at any point in the system yields a metric compounded of *cause* and *effect* simultaneously. If we open this loop anywhere, the value of this metric would change radically, and the system would cease to function as a system. We could, however, remove each element and measure its transfer function independent of the system, shutting down the system itself for a time. On the other hand, operating the system with its loop open would transform it into a nonsystem of overheated motors, blown fuses, and aimlessly drifting vehicle.

From the standpoint of systems analysis, it makes little difference whether the functional element is a human muscle, an electrical motor, or a hydraulic pump, so long as the other elements are compatible with it. Any element of a cybernetic system may be specified in terms of its transfer function.

It was Norbert Wiener who called to our attention the likelihood that advances in servomechanism technology pointed to fundamental feedback processes in natural organisms and elsewhere.[8] Although Ludwig von Bertalanfy has since attempted to make competing claims to the effect that cybernetics, servomechanism theory, and what he calls general systems theory were parallel developments,[9] it is clear that the technology was highly developed in both the United States and Britain prior to attempts to generalize them as applicable to other kinds of systems. Wiener and his colleagues applied them to a wide variety of physical, physiological, and neuromuscular systems in the early 1940s, although it was not until 1947 that they selected the term "cybernetics" to subsume them.[10] There is nothing of significance in von Bertalanfy's general systems theory that is not included in the earlier efforts in cybernetics.

From the standpoint of social theory, it is significant that Norbert Wiener resisted the efforts of Margaret Mead and other social scientists who sought to convince him to apply cybernetics to social phenomena. The problem, as he recounts it in the 1948 volume, was one involving a social scientist's inability to obtain long-term data under essentially constant conditions. Only if this were possible would it enable one to apply truly appropriate statistical techniques:

To begin with, the main quantities affecting society are not only statistical, but the runs of statistics on which they are based are excessively short. . . . For a good statistic of society, we need long runs *under essentially constant conditions*, just as for a good resolution of light we need a lens with a large aperture. The effective aperture of a lens is not appreciably increased by augmenting its nominal aperture, *unless the lens is made of a material so homogenous that the delay of light in different parts of the lens conforms to the proper designed amount by less than a small part of a wavelength. Similarly, the advantage of long runs of statistics under widely varying conditions is specious and spurious.* Thus, the human sciences are very poor testing grounds for a new mathematical technique: as poor as the statistical mechanics of a gas would be to a being of the order of size of a molecule, to whom the fluctuations which we ignore from a larger standpoint would be precisely the matter of greatest interest.[11]

This injunction against attempting a statistic of society did not discourage the efforts of social scientists bent on mathematical modes of expression, particularly on the American side of the Atlantic. Nor did it dissuade Talcott Parsons from at last claiming that his earlier delineation of a general system of action constituted a cybernetic system.[12]

In the discussion so far several important distinctions have been made regarding our understanding of action systems. Any action system (mousetrap, kite, judicial, servomechanism) must have discernible boundaries to its organization, setting it apart from the environment in which it is acting. Any element of the system, or any component or subsystem (rudder, amplifier, jury, snare), must similarly be specifiable. Systems may be of a recursive cause-and-effect variety (mousetraps, data-processing systems) or of the nonrecursive variety (servomechanisms, neuromuscular), in which change occurs throughout the system and modifies initiating causes by feedback processes.

A cybernetic system is a nonrecursive adaptive action system, employing one or more feedback loops or paths that modify in significant ways the functional performance of the system in its interaction with its environment. Its overall functioning may be specified in terms of its transfer functions and its environment. The elements or subsystems within it may also be specified in terms of their transfer functions, with the system serving as their environment. Transfer functions are specifiable in terms of the relationship of the output to the input of the component, subsystem, or system considered. These usually, although not necessarily, may be expressed in quantitative terms.

The actions one performs in picking up a pencil may be analyzed in accordance with the procedures outlined in the operation of the automatic pilot, with motors replaced by muscles and sensor replaced by eyes. As the hand (or vehicle) draws closer to the pencil (heading), feedback signals to the eye (sensor) result in increasingly smaller incremental changes throughout the system until the hand just touches the pencil, as in Figure 2.3c. Wiener relates how knowledge of the system processes shown in Figure 2.3 and their corresponding equations enabled him to predict the existence of a pathological condition in human action responses corresponding to that of Figure 2.3f of the servomechanism condition.[13] Ataxia of a type related to syphilis of the central nervous system known as *tabes dorsalis* corresponds to the condition of low feedback shown in Figure 2.3e:

However, an excessive feedback is likely to be as serious a handicap to organized activity as a defective feedback. In view of this possibility, Mr. Bigelow and myself approached Dr. Rosenblueth with a very specific question. Is there any pathological condition in which the patient, in trying to perform some voluntary act like picking up a pencil, overshoots the mark, and goes into uncontrollable oscillation? Dr. Rosenblueth immediately answered us that there is such a well-known condition, that it is called purpose tremor, and that it is often associated with injury to the cerebellum.[14]

This corresponds to the condition shown in Figure 2.3f. Cybernetic systems analysis is applicable to a wide variety of phenomena of a naturalistic kind.

A cybernetic system is distinguished from other nonrecursive systems in that it is a system of proportional control. An electronic data-processing system, such as those incorporating computers, terminals, discs, tapes, and related software and hardware is not such a control system. Although furnished with inputs and outputs in common with all systems that are not primarily classificatory, its functional imperatives involve only calculation, storage, and reproduction. Such feedback loops as it contains are only for the redundant operations performed in presenting data in the form required by human operators. It is essentially a mousetrap system that, once set in motion, passes through preprogrammed steps to some conclusions, at which time it must be reset. However, such data-processing systems may be incorporated as elements within control systems of sophisticated designs to assist in the processing of large bodies of information where the control function is highly complex (as, for example, in space vehicles requiring both on-board and ground-based calculations).[15]

Similarly, a high-fidelity sound reproduction system, whether it be stereophonic or monaural, is not such a proportional control system. Although it too may have various inputs for tapes, records, and the like, and various outputs for loudspeakers or recording heads and incorporate internal feedback networks to minimize distortion and to assure a wide range of response, it is not a system *interacting* with its environment. It is a reproduction system that only reiterates at high amplitudes of sound those acoustical patterns presented to it in acoustic or magnetic codings.

The interrelations of components in such systems as these may be specified diagrammatically, as in flow diagrams or schematic-wiring diagrams, similar to the specification of black boxes in control systems, and transfer functions for these may sometimes be written. But this treatment of the system as a *system* does not give it any distinctly nonrecursive cybernetic quality.

In specifying a cybernetic system as a control system, we impute to such a system the regulation of some activity or action. Hence a cybernetic system is essentially a nonrecursive (feedback) system in which information (signal) is processed to control that activity in which the system is interacting with its environment.[16]

It is this association of information with the determination of activity that has made the idea of a system so attractive to social theorists. Social systems are conceived by their analysts as systems of action. It is the antecedents and consequences of such actions which form the central concerns of sociologists and other social scientists. Parsons, for example, came close to the definition of a transfer function in cybernetic terms when he specified in the early pages of *The Social System* that his conception involved analysis of "the structure and processes of the systems built up by the relations of such units to their situations, including other units. It is not as such concerned with the *internal* structure of the units except so far as this directly bears on the relational system."[17] Black boxes have internal structures that are of no interest to us in our analysis of the overall system. What is of interest are the transfer functions performed by these black boxes, the functions they perform in their relations to all other elements comprising the action system.

Talcott Parsons did not originally conceive of his proposed analytical scheme as explicitly cybernetic. In the preface to his *The Social System* (1951) he tells us that it was L. J. Henderson who impressed on him the extreme importance of the concept of a system in scientific thought, and he credits Pareto with making the first frail steps in this direction.[18] The book itself is claimed to be an attempt to carry out Pareto's intention, but employing a "structural-functional level of analysis which is quite different from that of Pareto."

The structural-functional level of analysis has extensive roots in social theory. The sociological concept of function appears widely in the works of Émile Durkheim and that of his *Année* school followers. As employed by Parsons and many of his contemporary functionalists, it was derived primarily from the earlier work of British anthropologists Radcliffe-Brown and Bronislaw Malinowski, both of whom took certain exceptions to Durkheim's formulations.[19] It was, however, Parsons' most brilliant student, Robert K. Merton, who developed the concept completely from these beginnings.[20] Merton saw its relation to the mathematical formulation of function:

Since it was first introduced by Leibnitz, the word function has its most precise significance in mathematics, where it refers to a variable considered in relation to one or more other variables in terms of which it may be expressed or on the value of which its own value depends. This conception, in a more extended (and often more imprecise) sense, is expressed by such phrases as "functional interdependence," and "functional relations," so often adopted by social scientists. When Mannheim observes that "every social fact is a function of the time and place in which it occurs," or when a demographer states that "birth rates are a function of economic status," they are manifestly making use of the mathematical connotation, though the first is not reported in the form of equations and the second is. The context generally makes it clear that the term function is being used in this mathematical sense, but social scientists not infrequently shuttle back and forth between this and another related, though distinct, connotation, which involves the notion of "interdependence," "reciprocal relation" or "mutually dependent variations."[21]

This related meaning, involving interdependence, reciprocal relation, and mutually dependent variations, is most highly developed in the cybernetic idea of a function as we have been delineating it. Here too it unites with its mathematical scales. The final realization of this seems to have encouraged Parsons to claim cybernetic status for his analytical scheme in 1961,[22] although he had avoided it in 1951, when such analysis, widespread in the natural sciences and in technology, was relatively unknown to social scientists. Merton's definition of functions as "those observed consequences which make for adaptation or adjustment of a given system" can be seen to apply to the transfer functions of nonrecursive adaptive systems.[23]

The conception of society as a structured "thing" is, of course, either implied or expressed overtly in all social thought, including the pre-scientific. Whether it took the form of "the mystical body of Christ," the Roman *res publica* (the "public thing"), the *Leviathan* of Thomas Hobbes, or the "thing of its own kind" of Durkheim, ideas of society have always stressed some form of organization of its parts.

In proposing a structural-functional method of analysis applicable to a social system of a cybernetic kind, Parsons carefully distinguished between structure and function:

The concept of structure focuses on those elements of the system which may be regarded as independent of the lower amplitude and shorter time-range fluctuations in the relation of the system to its external situation. It thus designates the features of the system which can, in certain strategic respects, be treated as constants over certain ranges of variation in the behavior of other significant elements of the theoretical problem. The functional reference, on the other hand, diverges from the structural in the "dynamic" direction. . . . Functional considerations relate to the problem of *mediation* between two fundamental sets of exigencies: those imposed by the relative constancy of "givenness" of a structure and the environing situation external to the system.[24]

The structures may accordingly be seen as relatively fixed black boxes and the functional referents as those transfer functions mediating the internal processes of the system to permit the system to interact with its environment.

Having introduced a tripartite division of *social system*, *cultural system*, and *personality system*, each "an independent focus of the organization of the elements of the action system," Parsons noted in 1951 that although the action frame of reference was related to all three, on the level of theory he was then attempting, "they do not constitute a single system, however this might turn out to be on some other theoretical level." But in his later work this disclaimer is abandoned and the cybernetic nature of the system asserted.[25] The general system of action is now seen to contain "basic subsystems" that include the cultural, personality, and social systems related in turn to a behavioral system in contact with the environment. "The links between structure and dynamic effects of the system are the functional imperatives (pattern maintenance, integration, goal attainment, and adaptation), in that order of importance, from the viewpoint of cybernetic control."[26] A cybernetic system is envisioned, consisting of structures (elements, components, subsystems) performing functions (pattern maintenance, goal attainment, integration, adaptation) controlling activity. Such a system involves feedback processes: individuals are cultural products in behavioral systems in contact with physical environments, and they help create cultural products that may in turn become institutionalized at the social system level and thence be incorporated into personality systems leading on to behavioral systems that act in accordance with them, and so on. Values are created or voiced initially by concrete individuals and have structures erected around them through the efforts of a collectivity of individuals who socialize other personality systems to these values.[27] The overall action system is a nonrecursive adaptive system in which behavioral systems feed back into the major subsystems. These distinctly nonrecursive features are considered by Parsons only in the most general way, with little concern for the simultaneous presence within them of amalgams of causes and effects. At the macrosocial level of his greatest concern they are long-term processes, taking years, decades, or even centuries to complete a processing of some action by the system. But at the concrete, individual level, that of the interactions between and among individuals, such processes are immediate, short-term, and far less abstract. The description and experimental validation of these processes were initially instituted by Parsons with Robert F. Bales and others for the study of small groups, employing the same *instrumental* versus *expressive* binary oppositions that Parsons employs in developing the pattern variables.[28]

In black-box format, the gross elements or subsystems of this general system of action may be represented as shown in Figure 2.4. The arrows are in the direction "of cybernetic control" specified by Parsons in the quotation already given.

This system presents several epistemological problems. Our previous discussion of nonrecursive systems clearly defined the bounda-

Figure 2.4
The Parsonian System in Schematic Form

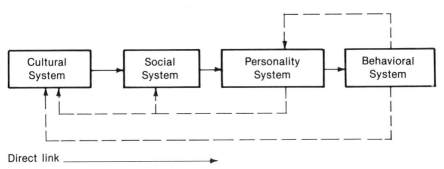

Direct link ⟶

Possible feedback loop paths ─ ─ ─ ─ ─ ─ ─ ─ ─ ─ ─ ─ ─ ⟶

ries between subsystems and elements. Here this is virtually impossible to do, and unless it is done, the possibility of being able to write anything approaching a transfer function is negligible. Parsons recognizes the problem of "boundary maintenance," asserting that theoretical and empirical differences exist for both the definition of structures (elements) and the processes internal to the system so far as our ability to specify the subsystems is concerned.[29] If they did not, he concluded, one subsystem could not be distinguished from the other. But this is a simple definitional fallacy. To state that differences must exist or we would not be able to specify hypothetical systems, as a means of legitimating their specification (and without specifying what such differences are), falls short of explanation. The boundary between, for example, the cultural system and the social system is more than a simple matter of "boundary maintenance," since both culture and society are not, strictly speaking, mutually exclusive categories unless one wishes to make them so by arbitrary definition. Parsons asserts by definition that values arise in the cultural system and have erected around them institutionalized structures that result in norms.[30] Thus values are "transmitted" or processed throughout the system, concrete individuals follow behavioral norms, and the Freudian emphasis later introduced into the system allows for all manner of non-normative behavior.

Although a behavioral system may "contain" a personality system, the social system and cultural system may not be so contained within a single behavioral system; they can exist there only in part. Therefore, the system as described cannot represent each ontologically unique behavioral system, of which there are many at any one time. "Behavior" is used here as a collective term, but "personality" cannot be so used, except in the most metaphorical sense (that is, as in "the French personality" or "the personality of the senate"). As described by Parsons, such things as personality and behavior are structured in ways and by processes unlike other processes present in the social and cultural systems. "Socialization" and "institutionalization" are not isomorphs, but contain distinctive features which, among other things, make it possible to specify the different subsystems in the first place. The system allows for such differences by the action of the functional imperatives, but the unit of analysis is confounded by the need to distinguish the boundaries of concrete individuals within the overall system.

Individuals are both personalities and organisms in interaction with others of their kind. The values and norms accordingly constitute "universalistic" structural categories that are particularistic only at the level of social roles.[31] Similarly, norms are specific to the role; hence role expectations involve values (shared normative components) and norms. Norms are "legitimated" by values, by culturally defined injunctions and imperatives.

It is clear that in all its patterned and recognizable forms, *behavior* is the *output* of the entire system envisioned by this general system of action. The equivalent of the information (or "signal") passing through the system are the *pattern variables*, polarized into *expressive* or *instrumental*, *rational*, or *nonrational* signals.[32] The *input* to the overall system is the formulation of expressive and instrumental signals from other behavioral systems operating in the same environment. The functional imperatives are the transfer functions of the black boxes that process these signals. They function to maintain patterns of institutionalized culture, to direct the attainment of specific goals among many possible goals, and to provide disposable facilities (such as money) associated with action generally. The mutual adjustment of the system's units or elements for the effective functioning of the overall system is the integrative function performed by the subsystem designated as the social system.[33]

Again we confront a certain problem here. In our delineation of adaptive, nonrecursive systems there was no need to introduce a black box performing an integrative function of this nature. Integrative functions are not necessary conditions for the existence of such cybernetic systems. The telic purposiveness or intentionality that otherwise integrates a conventional cybernetic system into a whole is supplied by an agency external to the system and located in the system's environment. Even mousetrap systems of a recursive kind are intentionally designed systems, with purposiveness imposed on them by their builders in the environment. It is clear that this cannot be the case in any system, cybernetic or otherwise, where agency is conceived as lying not in the environment but within the system itself. The only possible exception is life *itself*. But even here we must be cautious, for living subsystems (such as nerves, muscles, organs) are involved in larger living systems that function as their environments and they may not be typically removed from these environments for any length of time and continue to function.

Since Parsons is concerned with outlining a general system of action where such action is meaningfully oriented in the Weberian sense, the integrative function for mutual adjustment of the various elements is required to be located within the system and not within the environment. It is this *non*cybernetic feature that distinguishes Parsons' system from other systems of cybernetic control. The system of action that results produces behavior that is endogenously purposive and goal-oriented. The teleological basis of human action lies within the action system and is not external to it.[34] This latter assumption would have been unacceptable to Radcliffe-Brown, whose criticism of Durkheim's formulations of a functionalist nature rested on similar assumptions.[35]

By locating the integrative function within the system for internal mutual adjustment, "self-maintenance" is provided. The system not only maintains itself in its environment, in the manner of a compass-guided automatic pilot servosystem—translating environmental strains into functional performances—but also does a measure of internal housekeeping to minimize or obviate *internal* strains.

It is significant that these noncybernetic functions are located by Parsons in the social system, the very part of the system of action he seeks to explain. Explaining a system by invoking the cybernetic analogy, while incorporating into it noncybernetic features that enable it to perform its activity, is certainly at odds with the perspective on systemic explanation offered by Percy Bridgman and quoted in the epigraph introducing this book. The thing to be explained is left out of the explanation. Parsons here creates a kind of "Maxwell's demon," a ghost within the machine, which, itself inexplicable, allows for other explanations.

Thus, although Parsons' analytical scheme can be shown to incorporate cybernetic features, its constituitive elements are not themselves integral to the idea of a cybernetic system, and this system's conditions for stability or instability (social order or social disorder) do not depend on its being a cybernetic system. Its most significant features, and those that have elicited the greatest amount of controversy, are the integrative and system-maintenance functions of the social system subsystem. These are not integral to the idea of a cybernetic system but have been inherited from earlier functionalist concerns dealing with social order. Here Hobbes, Durkheim, and Weber converge. These features are therefore integral to the functioning of Parsons' general system of action since they directly address the classical question of sociological concern, How is society possible? It is clear that these elements cannot be removed from this scheme of action and the scheme remain useful for purposes of sociological analysis.

The intention here is not to criticize the Parsonian action system but to indicate the measure of fitness between it and the more general idea of cybernetic systems of action. Parsons has stressed repeatedly that his is a system useful for analysis of social phenomena of various kinds. Hence, the principles of organization which we seem to find within it are necessarily those we impose on it to increase our understanding in both utilitarian and pragmatic terms. Its internal organization is not determined by some intrinsic properties of the elements, but is an organization we impose for analytical purposes associated with understanding. The form and function of each element of the system is relatively fixed and is defined by Parsons in its relation to other contingent elements. Quite properly, these elements are not interchangeable, one with another.

Moreover, the system is not a simple, one-shot mousetrap requiring environmental factors to reset it for further operations. It is a continuously self-adjusting system responding to its environmental factors. It incorporates adaptive, nonrecursive features that result in widespread effects throughout the system in response to sensed conditions of the environment. That the goal direction leading to its theoretical development fails in its attempt to specify its most significant social feature is unfortunate. The possibility of a cybernetic approach to the problem of the structure and functions of societies has fascinated many social scientists. Thus, as late as 1963, J. J. C. Smart could assert:

Descartes thought that while animals were mere machines, men were machines with souls. As Ryle has put it, according to Descartes, man is a ghost in a machine. . . . But is there any reason why a machine should not have the sort of purposiveness, appropriateness and adaptiveness that is characteristic of human beings? I shall contend that we have no reason for thinking that a machine could not have the human sort of intelligence, and therefore that the antecedent scientific plausibility of physicalism should lead us to espouse the view that men are physical mechanisms. The hypothesis that I shall put forward is an old one in that it goes back to LaMettrie's *L'Homme Machine*, but it has been enormously strengthened by recent developments in cybernetics, the theory of self-regulating mechanisms.[36]

The cybernetic idea of a system may be seen as the most developed expression of mechanism attained by contemporary natural science. It continues to dominate large bodies of political, economic, and sociological thought, although its employment there is seldom other than metaphorical.[37] Although in technology it has enabled us to place men on the moon and send vehicles journeying to Jupiter and beyond, in the social sciences it does not appear to have been particularly productive. Norbert Wiener predicted, decades ago, who it would not be. And although it is still a favorite with econometricians, as the economy flounders it seems to have less salience than it did in more prosperous times.

The Parsonian system, transformed by the pressures within the discipline into a cybernetic system, is closest to the idea of a cybernetic system of society that the social sciences have managed to achieve. This transformation from one kind of system to another may have been a mistake, and theoreticians may have to return to Parsons' original formulation in the future.

Notes

1. Karl Mannheim, *Essays on the Sociology of Knowledge* (London: Routledge & Kegan Paul, 1968), p. 205.

2. D. C. Phillips, *Holistic Thought in Social Science* (Stanford, Calif.: Stanford University Press, 1976).

3. See D. C. Phillips, "The Methodological Basis of Systems Theory," *Academy of Management Journal* 15(4), 1972.

4. See Walter Buckley, *Sociology and Modern Systems Theory* (Englewood Cliffs, N.J.: Prentice-Hall, 1967), for a discussion of the applicability of contemporary systems theory to social phenomena.

5. This is Norbert Wiener's view in *Cybernetics* (New York: Wiley, 1948).

6. Note that if we consider the "man/machine" combination of Boy Scout/compass we have an adaptive, interactive system. One element of this system is the compass, another element is the Boy Scout. It is the Boy Scout's function, in this larger system, to provide the feedback by rotating the compass card periodically to maintain the needle above the N on the card. Thus, a mousetrap system may form a subsystem of an adaptive system.

7. The internal description of such a system requires the specification of the system by a set of n measures, called "state variables." Their change with time is expressed by a set of n simultaneous, first-order differential equations of the form,

$$dQ_n/dt = f_1, (Q_1, Q_2, Q_3, \ldots, Q_n)$$

which are equations of motion. This set of equations enables one to determine, among other things, whether the system is stable or not. See Ludwig von Bertalanfy, "The History and Status of General Systems Theory," *Academy of Management Journal* 15(4), 1972, esp. pp. 417ff.

8. Wiener, 1948.

9. Bertalanfy, 1972.

10. Wiener, 1948, p. 19.

11. Wiener, 1948, p. 34; italics in original.

12. Talcott Parsons, "An Outline of the Social System," in Talcott Parsons et al., *Theories of Society*, vol. 1 (New York: Free Press, 1961).

13. Wiener, 1948, p. 14.

14. Wiener, 1948, p. 15.

15. Again, as in note 6, above, this involves incorporating a mousetrap system—the data-processing computer—as a subsystem of a cybernetic system.

16. Note that in information theory it is Claude Shannon's binary switching logic that applies. This has recursive properties only. The communicative acts it treats are discrete events, not simultaneous functions of causes and effects. The best analogy is two persons communicating by telegraph. A sends B a message, then B sends A a message, and so on. They continue in the sequence A—B—C of Figure 8.1, not in the order of Figure 8.4 (see Chapter 8).

17. Talcott Parsons, *The Social System* (New York: Free Press, 1951), p. 4.

18. Parsons, 1951, p. vii.

19. Mark Abrahamson's *Functionalism* (Englewood Cliffs, N.J.: Prentice-Hall, 1978) contains a good discussion of the Radcliffe-Brown : Durkheim : Malinowski differences.

20. Robert K. Merton, *Social Theory and Social Structure* (New York: Free Press, 1957), pp. 19–82.

21. Merton, p. 21.

22. Parsons, 1961.

23. See Merton, 1957, p. 51.

24. Parsons, 1961, p. 36.

25. Parsons, 1961, p. 37.

26. Parsons, 1961, p. 37ff.

27. A system so conceived is able to accommodate a wide range of theoretical viewpoints other than its own. See George V. Zito, *Sociological Concepts* (New York: Irvington, 1975).

28. See Robert F. Bales, *Interaction Process Analysis* (Cambridge, Mass.: Addison-Wesley, 1950); *Personality and Interpersonal Behavior* (New York: Holt, Rinehart & Winston, 1970); Talcott Parsons and Robert F. Bales, *Family, Socialization, and Interaction Process* (New York: Free Press, 1955); Talcott Parsons, R. F. Bales, and Edward Shils, *Working Papers in the Theory of Action* (New York: Free Press, 1953); Talcott Parsons and Edward Shils, *Toward a General Theory of Action* (New York: Harper & Row, 1951).

29. Parsons, 1961, p. 36.

30. Parsons, 1961, p. 31.

31. Parsons, 1961, p. 42.

32. Parsons, 1961, pp. 35, 43.

33. Parsons, 1961, p. 38.

34. It is interesting to compare this aspect of Parsons' system with the intentional ordering of the syntagms in the Saussurian system, discussed in later chapters of this book. In the Saussurian system the actor's intentionality is exogenous to the system, not endogenous, as in the Parsonian system. This distinction is crucial for understanding the differences between the two systems.

35. See the discussion in Abrahamson, 1978, p. 38.

36. J. J. C. Smart, *Philosophy and Scientific Realism* (New York: Humanities Press, 1963), p. 107.

37. Manfred Stanley, *The Technological Conscience* (New York: Free Press, 1979).

Language as a System   3

Having reviewed the various arrangements constituting action systems, the question necessarily arises, Is language a system of the same kind as that which sociologists, whether they think in terms of recursive or nonrecursive models, consider society to be? To some this question may seem irrelevant. An immediate response is to claim that language is a classification system only, not an action system. Classical linguistics treated it as such. If one has ever suffered the bother of learning a foreign language in college, this classificatory aspect has been enhanced for him. There are certain classes of words, such as verbs denoting action and nouns denoting things, and a syntax and grammar regulating their usage. With a foreign language, we are required to memorize these things and haltingly place them into relationships with one another in order to use them. But this is not the way a native speaker of a language acquires and uses his language. Even uneducated persons have a mastery of their mother tongue that escapes many better-educated persons who have had to learn the language in other ways.

If a language is not our mother tongue, we usually find it easiest to read, more difficult to speak, and very difficult to write, since the need to follow the laws of the particular language becomes increasingly evident in this order. That a language is a system of some kind is evident enough: there are sets of relations among parts, between subject and predicate, nouns and the adjectives modifying them, adverbs, verbs, and certain kinds of clauses. That it is likely an action system is shown by its function in producing speech. If it is indeed an action system, its classificatory function may be only subsidiary.[1] If the classical sociological question is How is society possible? then the classical linguistics question should be How is language possible? Oddly enough, however, this was not the classical linguistics question, but arose only in the work of Ferdinand de Saussure.[2] Instead of questioning how language is possible, classical linguistics occupied itself for generations with classifications of word origins and specification of the relatedness of different language groups. Classical linguistics studied the historical development of languages, not the language system as it is employed at any one time by a user who attempts to articulate a set of meanings.

Saussure begins by specifying four pairs of major oppositions in his effort to specify the systemic nature of language:

1. The distinction between *langue* (literally a tongue or specific language) and *parole* (speech, or use)[3]
2. The distinction between signifier and signified[4]
3. The relation between synchronic and diachronic analyses[5]
4. The distinction between associative and syntagmatic relations[6]

All four bear directly on Saussure's understanding of the nature of language as a system:

* 1. *Langue vs. Parole*. It is important to distinguish between (a) the physical reality of speech (*parole*), articulated sounds performed in vocal acts, and (b) some language (*langue*), such as French or German, although both are generally understood as different manifestations of language generally (*langage*). Speech, or *parole*, is the active aspect of a language carried on by individuals—what Saussure calls "the executive phenomenon" (p. 13). The individual is always its master, for it is he who makes the physical sounds and gives them their reality in the object world. This is an activity carried on among concrete individuals communicating with one another.

A language (*langue*), however, is no such real activity. It is not a thing that is complete in the brain of any one speaker; it exists only within a collectivity (p. 14) that created it (p. 13). A language is there-

---

*Throughout this part of the discussion, the page citations refer to the English-language edition of Saussure's *Course in General Linguistics* (New York: McGraw-Hill, 1966).

fore one of several social institutions (p. 10) passively assimilated by the individual native speaker (p. 10) and requires no reflection or pre-meditation on his part while he is engaged in the act of speaking (p. 14). Language is a system of signs where each sign consists of two parts, a meaning and a sound image, both of which are psychological units. The *only* essential thing about language is this union of the two parts (p. 15).

Parole is individual; *langue*, however, is wholly social (pp. 5, 9, 10, 11), because it is collective in nature (pp. 11, 13, 14), a social fact (p. 6).

A language (*langue*), then, is a social system of psychological signs that a user employs when he engages in speech (*parole*).

2. *Signifier vs. Signified*. Psychological units comprise the elements of this system of signs. Each consists of a *meaning* (the signified) and a *sound image* (the signifier), and not of an object and our name for it (p. 66). This characteristic of the linguistic sign is crucial for Saussure. The property of language is not such that names are applied by it to objects in the world around us. If this were so, it would imply that language was simply a system of nomenclature, and to translate something from (say) French into English would require only the substitution of the appropriate word, a one-to-one mapping between elements of the two language systems. But the French language system is not the same as the English language system. The French and the English are not members of the same speech community (or collectivity or social system) and have not represented their worlds in the same way. Jonathan Culler gives a good example of this:

The sound sequences of *fleuve* and *rivière* are signifiers of French but not of English, whereas *river* and *stream* are English but not French. . . . The organization of the conceptual plane is also different in English and French. The signified *river* is opposed to *stream* solely in terms of size, whereas *fleuve* differs from *rivière* not because it is necessarily larger but because it flows into the sea, while a *rivière* does not. In short, *fleuve* and *rivière* are not signifieds or concepts of English. They represent a different articulation of the conceptual plane.[7]

This applies not only to single words but also to whole expressions. The sound image one articulates does not point to a thing; it points to a concept, a meaning, and these meanings differ among different language communities. It is the pairing of these meanings with sound images that constitutes linguistic signs such as words, parts of words, and entire expressions.

This pairing is arbitrary, since there is nothing in the sequence of sounds making up *river* (for example) that denotes the meaning it has for English-speaking people who employ it.[8] The letter sounds of *river* are not in any way dependent on the idea of a large stream of water located on land. The speech community could have evolved some other sound-image to go with this meaning. While there are certain exceptions to this general rule, as in the case of onomatopoeia, where sound and meaning are less arbitrary in their relation, these are clearly non-typical.

The signifier, then, is arbitrary, since some other sound-image could have been used to perform its function (or value), and its relation to what is signified is also arbitrary, for there is nothing in it that binds it to the concept or meaning, the signified.

A little consideration shows that this *signified* is also arbitrary. Saussure considers the ''8:25 p.m. Geneva-to-Paris'' train:

We feel that it is the same train every day, yet everything—the locomotive, coaches, personnel—is probably different. Or if a street is demolished, then rebuilt, we say that it is the same street even though in the material sense, perhaps, nothing of the old one remains. Why can a street be rebuilt and still be the same? Because it does not constitute a purely material entity; it is based on certain conditions that are distinct from the materials that fit the conditions.[9]

It is clear that what is signified is not an object thing but a set of relations or conditions, something on the psychological plane of meanings, and is arbitrary in its ontological status. Signifiers and signifieds have each an independent life; either or both are subject to change.

A language (*langue*), then, is a social system of psychological signs which is used by institutionally socialized individuals engaging in speech (*parole*). These signs each consist of a word-image, or *signifier*, and a *signified* mental concept united in an arbitrary relationship. Both are themselves arbitrary.

3. *Synchronic vs. Diachronic.* If a language is a system such as indicated by these first two considerations, then its component parts should be capable of definition in order that we may treat it as a system, functioning as a whole at any one time. We should be able to study its present organization and analyze it as we did mousetraps and kites.

Such a form of systems analysis is ahistorical; it treats the system as a *synchronic* whole, complete in itself.[10] This does not preclude *diachronic* or across-time analysis of the historical variety. Language systems do undergo historical changes; signifieds and signifiers change. Such diachronic analysis is what linguistics had traditionally concerned itself with, tracing word origins, common roots, and the like— what is usually referred to as *etymology*. It generally ignored *synchronic* analysis, analysis of a language system in its operative state at any *one time*. Thus, it ignored the question How is language possible? It is to such synchronic analysis that Saussure sought to direct attention.[11]

Synchronic linguistics, then, is "concerned with the logical and psychological relations that bind together coexisting terms and form a system in the collective mind of speakers," while diachronic linguistics studies only "those relations that bind together successive terms not perceived by the collective mind but substituted for each other without forming a system."[12]

The collective mind here is the sum of individual minds that coexist, not a metaphysical entity with its own memory. It is more Durkheimian than Jungian. It is not complete in any one individual mind; no one person understands *all* the language as it exists at one moment in its diachronic evolution. This collective nature is deemed very important by Saussure.

4. *Syntagmatic vs. Paradigmatic*. Saussure sees the need for two kinds of methods in performing the synchronic analysis of a language system. He terms these methods *syntagmatic* and *associative* (although in present usage the latter is usually termed *paradigmatic* analysis, a convention I will follow in common with other commentators).[13] The need for two different forms of analysis is based on the fact that two different kinds of mental activity are involved when we employ a language. One form is best illustrated by the use of the sentence. Whether spoken or not, a sentence includes a set of lineal relations among its elements. It occurs as a succession of parts, one sign following another in time. Such serial combinations of elements are *syntagms*.[14] A syntagm is always composed of two or more elements, as in "Now is the time" or "re-read" or "misuse." "In the syntagm, a term acquires its value only because it stands in opposition to everything that precedes or follows it, or both."[15] Here *value* is used in the sense of *function*. The term's lineal position is of the utmost significance. Thus,

the English sentence *The ball hits John* does not mean the same thing as the sentence *John hits the ball*. The term *John* acquires a different function or value as a consequence of its lineal position within the syntagm, as does *hits* or *ball*, although exactly the same set of elements is given in both cases. Therefore it is not the elements of the set that are conveying the *principal meaning in the sentence*; it is the set of relations among these elements in their sequencing. The number of permutations of this particular set of elements is limited, although in American slang the construction *Ball hits the John* is remotely possible, but *The hits John ball* is not, and so on. The syntagmatic is one form of activity we engage in mentally when we wish to convey meaning. We cannot speak or think two terms or elements simultaneously, but must order them one after another in real time. As I type this or as you read this, we both must move along the lines of letters to unravel what is here. This is a syntagmatic activity.

The other form of mental activity we engage in is not locked into this lineality, this sequencing. When you read *ball* in the sentence *John hits the ball*, there is a kind of vertical process at work along with the horizontal lineality. This is much more difficult to specify. When you read *ball*, a host of associated words and meanings are also involved. *Ball* is distinguished from *bell*, *boll*, *bull*, and *bill*. There is a relation here in terms of the possible intermediate vowel and the images associated with them. But in addition, *ball* is not the signifier of one particular signified. *Ball* may signify a spherical play object concept or the concept of a formal party. And what precisely is signified by the expression *Let's have a ball?* Not a highball, not the plaything, not the dance party, but something quite unlike them. Similarly, if a male acquaintance should say, "I'd love to ball her," a decidedly different mental image is evoked. Thus, quite apart from the property of lineality or serial ordering in determining meaning, there is this other property, which excludes alternate meanings. There is a determination of what is *not* present, what is absent. "The syntagmatic relation is *in praesentia*. It is based on two or more terms that occur in an effective series. Against this, the associative (or *paradigmatic*) relation unites terms *in absentia* in a potential mnemonic series."[16]

A language is a social system of psychological signs which individuals use to engage in speech activity. Each sign consists of a word-image or *signifier* and a *signified* or meaning united in an arbitrary relationship. The signifier and signified are themselves arbitrary. A language system exists as a synchronic whole of interrelated elements. These function in two ways in *parole*: by their relations one-to-the-other in their lineal sequencing (the syntagmatic relation) and by the sets of associated elements they exclude from expression by their presence (the paradigmatic relation).

Saussure's repeated claim that this system is a social system does not present a problem, because the collective character of a language is clearly apparent. Saussure calls it "a social fact," precisely what Durkheim would have called it.

Is the system as we have described it an action system? An action system, we saw, has activity as its primary function, unlike nonaction systems, which reproduce, calculate, classify, and so forth. It is clear that *parole* is an activity, whether the discourse be spoken or written.[17] *Parole* is also the sole output of the system, the behavioral product of the mental processes involved when the individual employs the syntagmatic and paradigmatic relations of the signs (each a paired meaning and sound-image) in an attempt to express "what's on his mind." His ability at such expression is clearly a function of the extent to which he has assimilated or acquired the institutionalized forms of his collectivity's language system.[18] These forms are not themselves entities in the usual sense. It is not the *names* of objects and the rules for connecting them that he has acquired. It is a set of differences that enable him to act out serially in speech "what's on his mind." The activity he performs is a product of those differences and hence a product of this system. A language is accordingly a kind of action system.

While it is clear that it is an action system, controlling an activity that takes place in an environment, what we customarily understand as *action* involves only that sequencing of events defined in Saussurian terms as the syntagmatic. Events follow upon events, as words follow upon words in a sentence, whatever the causal connections, or lack of causal connections, between events. Even a cybernetic system, for all its nonrecursive processes where effects modify causes, involves sequential activity directed toward some end other than itself, such as the alignment of a vehicle with a directional vector. Whether this occurs as a smooth asymptotic process or an overshoot and possible oscillation, the behavior of the system as a whole may be plotted as a function of linear time. This is a specification of a syntagmatic variety. Similarly, when Parsons refers to "a direction of cybernetic control" passing from the cultural system to the social system and then to the personality system, his understanding of the overall process is that it is syntagmatic. The significance and nature of paradigmatic processes in shaping the activity is also present in the Parsonian system. These are the (unspecified) transfer functions that effectively process, modify, and change that which is flowing syntagmatically through the system ''in the direction of cybernetic control.'' In both the automatic pilot system and the Parsonian action system, there is a set of signals being processed by black boxes whose transfer functions directly affect the condition of these signals. The black boxes in the Parsonian system are institutionalized into more or less permanent structures, often exceeding the lifetimes of the individuals whose behaviors are the controlled features they seek to explain.

In the Saussurian system something quite different is taking place. The institutionalized forms do not exist apart from the things being processed. These are one and the same—the linguistic signs. There are no black boxes, as in other nonrecursive action systems, through which signals flow to be processed. Black box and signal are combined here in the linguistic sign itself. This is partially a consequence of the dual nature of the sign, the fact that it consists of both a sound-image and a meaning, paired together. But it is largely a consequence of the arbitrary nature of the sign and the fact that it does not point to anything. It contains meaning only to the extent that it has a paradigmatic status involving differences between it and all other signs to which it is related. So there is no ''stuff'' to be processed by ''something else.'' No substance is involved, in this sense. ''The elements of sound and thought combine;'' Saussure asserts on p. 113, ''their combination produces a form, not a substance.'' [19]

Action systems, whether of the mousetrap variety or the interactive variety, are internally organized to some desired end. This implies some telic principle directing the processes, whether it be internal (as in the Parsonian system) or external (as in the mousetrap) to the system itself. A control system controls to some end. These are therefore rationally ordered systems with components organized according to the functions they perform. Although they may sometimes produce unanticipated consequences of their purposive activity, in Merton's sense, their rational status remains unimpaired despite such latent functions.

The language system, however, is not such a rationally ordered system, at least not in the form presented by Saussure—and he is quite specific on this point:

> Everything that relates to language as a system must, I am convinced, be approached from this viewpoint, which has scarcely received the attention of linguists: the limiting of arbitrariness. This is the best possible basis for approaching the study of language as a system. In fact, the whole system of language is based on the irrational principle of the arbitrariness of the sign, which would lead to the worst sort of complication if applied without restriction. But the mind contrives to introduce a principle of order and regularity into certain parts of the mass of signs, and this is the role of relative motivation. If the mechanism of language were entirely rational, it could be studied independently. Since the mechanism of language is but a partial correction of a system that is by nature chaotic, however, we adopt the viewpoint imposed by the very nature of language and study it as it limits arbitrariness.[20]

If the language system is an action system, it is of a form we have not encountered elsewhere. Although it bears a superficial resemblance to such systems as Parsons' general system of action and to classificatory systems such as the periodic table of elements, a closer examination reveals significant differences. These include the integration of both syntagmatic and paradigmatic properties within the elements themselves, that is, within *each* element. The result is that what these elements perform as functions are consequences not of any intrinsic property of their own but of the sets of differences they specify among a chaotic universe of elements, the linguistic signs. In short, the ordering of the system, such as it is, does not conform to some purposive rational principle. Ordering of signs along some rational dimension takes place only as *parole* articulates the meanings it constructs from the syntagmatic and paradigmatic possibilities present in the system. The mind of the user selects and produces combinations of the differences it knows exist among the elements, and thus intentionally orders its meanings. It does this by continually presenting oppositions in combinatory form. Moreover, it does this independently of the real existence of object forms in the environment within which it operates.

The signifier *mermaid* in English is not an empirically derived consequence of observation of the object world, but comes into existence only as a syntagmatic possibility of sounds and meanings arbitrarily related. It becomes clear that once this kind of system is specified as that employed by language, nothing in the world of objects may be mapped, one-to-one, by language to itself in a positive fashion. Language cannot dictate, by axiomatic logical forms or syllogisms, any "truth" related to anything but itself. This has led one American structuralist to assert, "The problematic of structuralism can be stated in straightforward terms: metaphysics is dead. Language and discourse have entered. Knowledge is only at the juncture of language as it is practiced and language as it is structured by social (hence historic) convention."[21]

The telic principle in language is accordingly not a property of the system itself, but is external to it. The intentionality of the user supplies the input and organizes an irrational system of elements into a rational, meaningful discourse. The output of the system is a series of meaningless sounds that are useful only to another person sharing the same social collectivity, who can approximate the meanings the speaker intends. A peculiarity of the Parsonian system as a cybernetic system was that the telic principle was internal to the system and not external, as in other action systems of a cybernetic variety. The Saussurian system is clearly not a cybernetic system, although a speaker's auditory sensations of his own sound-making may enable him to enunciate more clearly. This means, however, that there are cybernetic physiological subsystems in the individual, not in the language. Nor is the language system a kind of recursive mousetrap system, for such action systems are wholly syntagmatic or sequential. The language system is an action system of its own kind, a thing *sui generis*, as Durkheim would say.[22] It is a social system, but it seems to be of a kind other than that envisioned by Parsons and by social scientists in general.

This idea of a system has profound implications for the social sciences and the humanities. It challenges our assumptions about how we think, speak and act. In the social sciences its implications are particularly challenging because it raises the likelihood that we have unwittingly become ensnared by the language we use and that what we claim to be "facts" and "truth" are only properties of a system that may not be mapped to an object world. We may have become trapped in a semiological cage.

Notes

1. Saussure also considers language classificatory, but when he treats it as a system this aspect is neglected and an action system results. See Ferdinand

de Saussure, *The Course in General Linguistics* (New York: McGraw-Hill, 1966), p. 9ff.

2. See note 6, Chapter 1.
3. Saussure (1966) defines *langue* on pp. 9–11 and *parole* on p. 13.
4. Saussure, 1966, pp. 65–66.
5. Saussure, 1966, pp. 79ff.
6. Saussure, 1966, pp. 122–27.
7. Jonathan Culler, *Ferdinand de Saussure* (Baltimore: Penguin, 1976), p. 15.
8. Saussure, 1966, p. 67.
9. Saussure, 1966, p. 108.
10. Saussure, 1966, p. 101.
11. Saussure, 1966, p. 103.
12. Saussure, 1966, p. 100.
13. Saussure, 1966, pp. 122ff.
14. Saussure, 1966, p. 123.
15. Saussure, 1966, p. 123.
16. Saussure, 1966, p. 123.
17. However, Saussure (1966) clearly makes the distinction that written language constitutes another system of signs, related to and derived from the first system.
18. Saussure, pp. 10, 14.
19. Saussure, 1966, p. 113.
20. Saussure, 1966, p. 133.
21. Charles C. Lemert and Willard A. Nielsen, Jr., "Structures, Instruments, and Reading in Sociology," in Ino Rossi, ed., *Structural Sociology* (New York: Columbia University Press, 1982), p. 329.
22. Durkheimian sociology is synchronic rather than diachronic in its analysis, stressing system rather than historical processes. But Durkheimian synchronic analysis does lend itself to diachronic concerns, as Durkheim's own distinction between mechanical and organic solidarity indicates. Kai T. Erikson applied a variety of Durkheimian synchronic analysis to the cases studied in his *Wayward Puritans* (New York: Wiley, 1966), although the historical span was limited. A more ambitious project employing such synchronic analysis to a broad historical phenomenon is Ephraim Mizruchi's *Regulating Society: Marginality and Social Control in Historical Perspective* (New York: Free Press, 1983).

Measuring Meanings   4

The peculiar status of the Saussurian language system as an action system derives from the irrational, arbitrary nature of the signifier. This makes possible a wide range of paradigmatic relations that get carried along, so to speak, in the syntagms as they become serially ordered and articulated. Saussure makes it clear that the speaker does not simply select a word to use because it signifies what he wants to say.[1] The idea the speaker wishes to express does not evoke a singular denotative quantum of any kind. It invokes a whole latent series of chains that makes possible the necessary oppositions for the formation of the sign one finally selects. By itself, the sign would have no signification if it did not pose oppositions of various kinds to other signs included in the system and excluded by its employment. Although linguistic signs are words and parts of words, in selecting a sign one does not select a *thing*, but selects instead the set of associative relations it allows in its sound-image and meaning components. Thus the linguistic signs have structured with them, in their oppositions, other sounds as well as other meanings, and paradigmatic functions are coupled to both.

Figure 4.1, which is similar to several furnished by Saussure in his *Course*, gives us some indication of this.[2] The syntagm *misfit* is articulated from the *m* end to the *t* end in real time. There are two sound images associated with the syntagm: the sounds written in English as *mis* and as *fit*, and two sets of meanings and their associative relations. A few of these are shown in Figure 4.1, but others branch off from each of these in treelike fashion. *Fit* means "proper," "belonging,"

Figure 4.1
Syntagmatic vs. Paradigmatic Dimensions

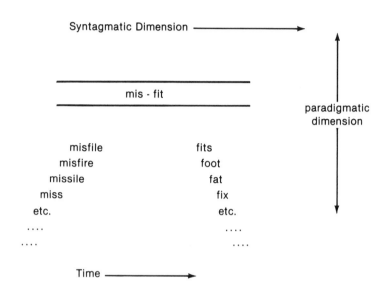

"tantrum," "appropriate," while *foot* means "twelve inches," "lower appendage," "pay for," and so on. The *mis-* as a prefix means nothing by itself, but it may mean "wrong," or "out of," or "inappropriate." But what does it mean in "missile," or "mischief," "mister," "miss," "missus"? Somehow only one sound sequence is performed in pronouncing the sign *mis-*, and like *fit* it does not directly signify anything by itself. It requires before it or after it other sound sequences that determine its functional quality or meaning. (She is the miss that I miss, Mister.)

Here we see clearly the arbitrariness of the signifier. Hence, when we employ such signifiers we must employ others with them so that out of the chaotic amalgams of paradigmatic relations *we* impose an order that we as users wish to convey to some other user. The other "reads" this order to decode the possible meaning we intend. When we are born into a language system, we know how to perform these highly complex operations without thinking about it. There is literally insufficient time for a recourse to some mental dictionary of words. What we do is select the sets of associative relations we have memorized in our lifetime and find intersections among them. It is at such mentally encoded intersections that one "finds" the appropriate sequential series of syntagms that spell out meanings. Only in this way are meanings articulated through words. The appropriate word springs into consciousness at the same time as one articulates it in speech or writing, a consequence of the intersections within memory of the sets of relationships, on the conceptual plane, of one's language. A moment's reflection shows that if this were not so, I would not be able to type these lines, for there is not present in my consciousness that thing I say prior to my saying (or typing) it. A moment ago, I did not know that I would write this line.

One further example: the English words corresponding to the sound images *tu* and *thair* present problems not only to those who have had to learn English as a second language but also to many native speakers. The difference is clearly specified in the written signs but indistinguishable in the spoken signs. There are *too*, *two*, and *to*, and *their*, *there*, and *they're*. Generations of English teachers have fumed over student papers abusing the distinctions in signifiers and signifieds of these words. From the standpoint of the present discussion, the problem is compounded because *to* is also used as a prefix (*to*day, *to*night, *to*ward) as well as a component of such words as *to*ol, *to*ast, or *to*mb. This is also true, but in a more limited way, of *there*. Here we see clearly that it is only the relations between these sound-images and others used with them that specifies their meanings. Whether the sound *tu* in English means *also*, a numeral, or the preposition for the equivalent of the dative case must be specified by other signs employed with it.

Again, we see that the language system is not rationally ordered internally, but chaotic. Some linguistic signs are positively arbitrary in this way, while some others are only relatively so.[3]

In stating that the appropriate word springs into consciousness at the same time as one articulates it in speech or writing, we are saying that the actual process of choosing intersections in memory is an unconscious, or at most semiconscious, process. Despite the reprimands of grandparents, we most often cannot "think before we speak," for there simply is not the time, and when there is we usually do not think out possible sentences to say. If the process becomes overly conscious we have difficulty performing it, for we do not consciously understand how we go about doing it "in our heads"; in such cases, we may find ourselves "at a loss for words."

This unconscious process has implications for other systems of a social nature modeled on the language system. Lévi-Strauss has been quick
to exploit these implications, as we shall see. But first I would like to
clear up some other problems associated with this peculiar kind of action system.

The representation of a signifier in the form shown in Figure 4.1 is
misleading. First, in specifying the sets of relations involved in the determination of the syntagm *misfit*, I have shown some signifiers located closer to it than others and in addition have not exhausted all the
possibilities. While it is probable that proximity in either sound-image
or meaning is significant in the process by which the mind selects an
appropriate signifier, this is not a given condition of the system as
Saussure presents it to us. Second, while the dimension designated as
the syntagmatic is clearly monotonic, since it is a function of the inevitable progression of time, the various possible sets of relations within
the paradigmatic dimension do not all exhibit the same quality or value.
Some are related by sound, some by meaning, and these are not always the same sound or same meaning. Thus the paradigmatic dimension may only be approximated in any schematic representation. Actually, the syntagmatic represents a bundle or cluster of signs related
in various ways and therefore lying along many dimensions, in a space
compounded of images of sounds and "shades" of meanings. This
implies that when one employs a language system he searches for differences in a multidimensional matrix of some kind. This search is
psychological, of course. And just as the language system, by virtue
of its social origins, connects directly to anthropology and sociology,[4]
so too it connects to social psychology:

We have just seen that language is a social institution; but several features set
it apart from other political, legal, etc. institutions. . . . Language is a system of signs that express ideas, and is therefore comparable to a system of
writing, the alphabet of deaf mutes, symbolic rites, etc. But it is most important of all these systems. A science that studies the life of signs within society
is conceivable; it would be part of social psychology and consequently of general psychology; I shall call it *semiology* (from the Greek *semeion*, "sign").[5]

It is this grounding of language in specifiable signs of a social nature
that has made language so appealing as a model for investigations in
disciplines other than linguistics, particularly in the social sciences.

Social psychology, often quite independently of Saussurian linguistics and at times in defiance of it, has made repeated excursions into linguistic phenomena.[6] Although semiology (or semiotics) is not clearly distinguished from semantics in social psychology, for Saussure semantics studies only *changes* in meaning, a diachronic phenomenon.[7] In social psychology this generally is not the case, and some social psychologists refer to a "semantic space" that is a meaning space similar to that existing only synchronically in the Saussurian system. Some of this research is interesting in light of our present discussion, because it furnishes possible clues to the manner in which access is made to a multidimensional matrix of meanings such as that implied in the Saussurian idea of a system.

Charles Osgood and his associates developed the now widely known *semantic differential* based on empirical findings. It has been used with success by a number of independent investigators.[8] The semantic differential seeks to measure the meaning of an object to an individual.[9] It suggests that many common words in English are bundles of meanings that may be ordered about three principal dimensions: *evaluation*, corresponding to the favorable-unfavorable dimension of conventional test instruments; *potency* or power; and *activity*. Test scales are constructed embodying these dimensions, and respondents are asked to evaluate some word, issue, or event along each scale. The results may then be plotted in a three-dimensional space and the subjects' responses compared. More significantly, the responses of various groups of individuals may thus be evaluated. For example, Figure 4.2 illustrates how one group of college students may evaluate such concepts as drugs, marijuana, laws, and crime based on a plotting of their mean scores on semantic differential scales.[10]

Figure 4.2 shows the mean responses of one social group tested (e.g., *males*, or *lower working class*, etc.).The same series of test scales can then be applied to other social groups (*females*, *middle class*, etc.), and the differences in the clusterings of the concepts in this semantic space can be directly compared for the two groups. This makes available a direct measure of the various signifieds evoked by identical signifiers for different sociocultural groups.

Although not intended by its inventors, the semantic differential appears to relate to Saussure's understanding of the language system in several different ways. First, it implies that access to the set of differences existing among signifiers does indeed occur along dimensions or

Figure 4.2

Semantic Space

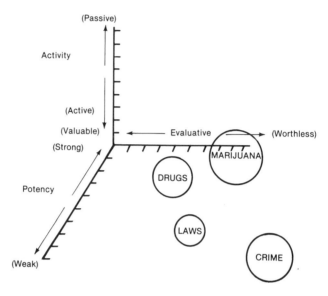

components of meaning. Some of these lie along Osgood's dimensions of *potency*, *evaluation*, and *activity* (among others) with sufficient salience to be readily tapped. Second, the relative completeness of the system, and the degree to which its relations are meaningful, varies within individuals and among groups sharing the same speech community, but these differences are measurable. The variation is social, as Saussure understood it to be. Moreover, it is able to present its findings in the form of differences among linguistic signs, rather than the signs themselves, and these correspond to differences in meaning. For example, in Figure 4.2, although it is of some interest that this group scores *crime* highly negative in evaluating this sign, it is more significant that its distance from *marijuana* is greater than its distance from *drugs*, that *drugs* are perceived as more valuable than *laws* and also stronger than *laws*, and so on. The results, in this form, allow us to perceive how it is possible for three or more meanings to be bound within one signifier in varying degrees and how various signifieds may relate to one another.

The semantic differential makes available a social-psychological instrument that inadvertently demonstrates that the system proposed by Saussure is not to be dismissed as lacking empirical justification. It demonstrates that individuals find in linguistic signs not things in themselves but sets of relationships composed of various components of meaning. And third, the relative arbitrariness of the signifiers is shown to vary widely.[11]

Experimental evidence of another kind is also available. This too helps us understand how such a system is accessed by its users. A. K. Romney and R. D'Andrade performed social-psychological experiments in which respondents were asked to select, among cards inscribed with English-American kinship terms, the pairs of terms most related to each other. The highest frequency of pairings occurred among such terms as father/son, mother/daughter, father/mother, and so on; the lowest frequencies occurred among such pairings as mother/son and father/daughter.[12] Roger Brown extended the work of Romney and D'Andrade to include such kin terms as uncle, aunt, and nephew.[13] The correlation in association performed by Romney and D'Andrade results in the two-dimensional representation shown in Figure 4.3a; Brown's extension in the three-dimensional representation is shown in Figure 4.3b.

Figure 4.3b shows that eight kin terms have been specified by three binary axes: sex, lineality, and generation. Brown points to the economy of this structure in its ability to specify meanings in terms of components and their relations. Certain other assumptions about the relatedness of social roles may also be deduced.[14]

Here again we are granted a clue, similar to that furnished by Osgood and his associates, to the way signifiers are employed. A set of three dimensions of meaning, quite independent of Osgood's *potency*, *evaluation*, and *activity*, result in the specification of a structure of signifiers within the language matrix. This illustrates our earlier observation that the syntagmatic represents bundles and clusters of signs in various ways and accordingly lying along many dimensions in a space compounded of mental images of sounds and possible meanings, a multidimensional matrix that does not lend itself completely to specification in analytical terms.[15] What both Osgood and Brown seem to indicate by their research is that when we are called upon to employ a language in some way we intentionally "shoot" a line of consciousness, here specified as dimensions of meaning such as sex, generation, potency, evaluation, and so on, through the learned set of relations

Figure 4.3
English-American Kinship Terms

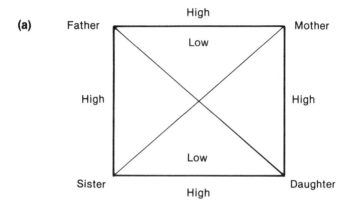

(a)

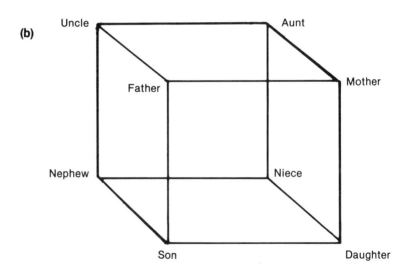

(b)

linking signifiers and find appropriate signifiers clustering about this "line." That we can repeatedly arrive at the same or similar signifiers shows that a language system is structured in terms of its meaning relations. Some of that structuring, albeit only an infinitesimal part, is evident in the examples drawn from the works of Brown and Osgood. The representation of this structure in spatial terms of orthogonal axes cannot be mistaken for the mnemonic structure, the existence of which is wholly mental. Nevertheless, a certain consistency in meanings is indeed present in such a geometric presentation. For example, we think of mothers as "above" daughters, as "closer" to their sisters (aunts) than to their nephews, and as of the same "kind" as their daughters, rather than their sons. In other words, the presentation implies other sets of relations we find consistent with our ideas of family structure and the roles and norms associated with that structure in English. Moreover, we are led to suspect that such redundancy in arriving at the same signifiers as a consequence of the system's structuring points to the phenomenon of intersubjectivity without fully explaining it. For if the language system is a system that consists of sets of relationships, rather than of signs that themselves possess meanings, then what one communicates by employing *parole* are these relationships and not the denotation of any object thing. Mind here communicates with mind because both individuals, speaker and hearer, have assimilated the same language system, and for no other reason. Thus, in its avoidance of imputing any relation whatever between signified and external object, but its insistence that the signifier and the signified exist in an arbitrary relation not grounded on the object world but grounded instead on its own system, Saussure's theory rejects entirely both the notion of an essence and the problem of intersubjectivity. The idea of a Platonic essence is inimical to such a system. A *thing* here is what it is only by virtue of a set of relations that gives it meaning, a meaning determined not by any quality of its own nor by any one signifier, but by the relation of this signifier to other signifiers. French structuralist Jacques Derrida dismisses all existentialism and phenomenology as the last futile and desperate gasps of a misguided logocentrism.[16] A thing cannot be a thing in and of itself; it is defined only *by what it is not*, within a system of signs quite independent of its own existence. Enculturation, socialization, and education to this system of signs and to its method of access allow for some measure of mutual understanding among members of the same collective speech group. Each member of this group performs the same mentalistic operations on the set of signifiers as fellow members, and it is this set of signs that creates the meanings they interchange, not something located in the objects of the physical world. The problem becomes a social-psychological one, a linguistic one, a concern of the social sciences, not the concern of metaphysics or metascience that Nagel specifies in the second epigraph opening this book. From this standpoint, it was inevitable that when philosophy finally returned to language it found there only varieties of games played by their own rules.

When Lévi-Strauss discusses the avunculate he performs a variety of analyses of kinship terms similar to those of Roger Brown. Brown's discussion is interesting in that it shows how users perform a variety of intellectual manipulations associated with the structure of the family. It was the result of research not connected with Saussure's assumptions. In the case of Lévi-Strauss, however, the structuralist agenda is assumed from the first.

Lévi-Strauss cites the work of Nicholas Troubetzkoy as an inspiration for his method of analysis.[17] He asserts that Troubetzkoy succeeded in reducing Saussure's approach to four basic operations:

1. Shift from a concern with the study of conscious linguistic phenomena to that of unconscious linguistic phenomena.
2. Do not treat terms as independent entities, but take the relations between them as the basis of analysis.
3. Employ the idea of a system; phonemes should disclose some concrete phonemic system and its structure.
4. Determine the laws that give this structure its absolute character, employing both inductive and deductive procedures.[18]

All these operations are invoked in the idea of a system we have derived from Saussure's *Course*. Lévi-Strauss's goal here is not to explicate the entire "phonemic system" of some language, but only one system, or subsystem, within it, one pertaining to the relationship existing between male child and mother's brother in many different cultural systems.

Radcliffe-Brown had shown that the avunculate covered two antithetical systems of attitudes. In cultural groups where the relationship between father and son is an easy, familiar one, the relationship of that son to his maternal uncle is one of dutiful respect. But in cultural groups where it is the father who merits this dutiful respect, the maternal uncle is treated by the son with familiarity. Radcliffe-Brown had concluded that in patrilineal societies such as the latter, the maternal uncle is treated as a kind of male mother, but that in the former system where descent is matrilineal there is no need for such a male mother. Here the opposite situation occurs: authority and respect are vested in the maternal uncle, and familiarity results between son and father. What strikes Lévi-Strauss is that two pairs of oppositions are being specified. This is more interesting than the fact that, as he reminds us, Radcliffe-Brown was wrong; not all matrilineal systems invest the uncle with authority, and not all patrilineal systems are of the type described. Either way, the avunculate is not found in all cultures, whatever their pattern of descent.[19]

Lévi-Strauss examines the kinship structure of the Trobriand Islanders, the Tonga, the Cherkess, and others and finds that different forms of the avunculate can exist whatever the type of descent.[20] He finds it a mistake to treat the avunculate diachronically and shows that only a synchronic analysis of the relations constituting the system makes the avunculate intelligible:

In order to understand the avunculate we must treat it as one relationship within a system, while the system must be considered as a whole in order to grasp its structure. This structure rests upon four terms (brother, sister, father, son) which are linked by two pairs of correlative oppositions in such a way that in each of the two generations there is always a positive relationship and a negative one. . . . This structure is the most elementary form of kinship that can exist. It is, properly speaking, *the unit of kinship*.[21]

Lévi-Strauss states the avunculate as a general relational law: ''The relation between maternal uncle and nephew is to the relation between brother and sister as the relation between father and son is to that between husband and wife.''[22]

This is a startling find in light of the path we have been following. Quite independently of Roger Brown, and without at all realizing the implications in Brown's American social-psychological terms, Lévi-Strauss is here asserting the set of *geometric* relations evident in the three-dimensional representation Brown makes of English-American kin terms, which we show in our Figure 4.3b. If we let the relation between maternal uncle and nephew be designated as A, that between brother and sister as B, that between father and son as C, and that between husband and wife as D, then Lévi-Strauss is asserting that A : B :: C : D (A is to B as C is to D). In the diagram of kin terms in Figure 4.3b, this results in the relations shown in Figure 4.4. A complete "fit" occurs between the Brown geometric representation and Lévi-Strauss's "general relational law" that satisfies a law of geometry. The relations specified as A and B by Lévi-Strauss's law are found to be diagonals of the Brown representation, while his C and D are both sides. Therefore, the relation A : B : : C : D holds. This resulting identity, based on two quite different theoretical approaches obtained by independent investigators, certainly merits serious consideration.

Lévi-Strauss mentions his "law" only in passing; he is more interested in the significance of the maternal uncle in terms of the incest taboo, which need not concern us here. What is significant is his application of semiotics to structures in social organization employing Saussurian theory. The signifiers *brother*, *sister*, *father*, and *son* specify attitudes in accordance with sets of relations that move beyond language. It could be argued that what he is doing here is treating the system of family relations *as if* it were identical with the language system.

The kinship system is a language; but it is not a universal language, and a society may provide other modes [than kinship] of expression and action. From the viewpoint of the anthropologist this means that in dealing with a specific culture we must always ask a preliminary question: Is the system systematic?

Figure 4.4

Lévi-Strauss's Avunculate
in Brown's Kinship Space

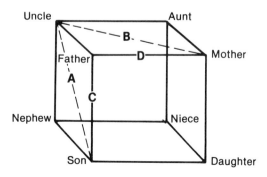

Such a question, which seems absurd at first, is absurd only in relation to language; for language is the semantic system par excellence; it cannot but signify, and exists only through signification. On the contrary, this question must be rigorously examined as we move from the study of language to the consideration of other systems which also claim to have semantic functions but whose fulfillment remains partial, fragmentary or subjective, like, for example, social organization, art and so forth.[23]

It is clear that the intention of Lévi-Strauss here is not metaphorical use but literal use. *The kinship system is a language.* Any system that lays a claim to signification of meaning is a language and may be treated in accordance with Saussurian theory.

Lévi-Strauss takes up the challenge posed by Saussure in the *Course.* In Lévi-Strauss's inaugural address on assuming the Chair of Social Anthropology at the College of France in 1960, he pays due respect to Saussure but argues that the latter did not fully understand—or at least his editors Charles Bally and Albert Sechehay did not understand—the true character of the phoneme.[24] This only emerged, he says, with Roman Jakobson and Nicholas Troubetzkoy. Similarly, he believes that the distinction between the synchronic and diachronic is too severe, since Saussure claimed that the diachronic does not belong to the collective mind. Thus,

De Saussure appears to deny the existence of a structure where it is not immediately given; Radcliffe-Brown confirms such an existence but, locating it in the wrong place (in the empirical), deprives the notion of structure of its full force and significance. In anthropology, as in linguistics, we know today that the synchronic can be as unconscious as the diachronic. . . . The *Course in General Linguistics* sets forth relations in equivalence between the phonetic, the diachronic and the individual which pertain to speech (*parole*); and the grammatical, the synchronic and the collective which pertain to language (*la langue*). But we have learned from Marx that the diachronic can also exist in the collective and from Freud that the grammatical can be achieved entirely within the individual.[25]

What Lévi-Strauss is saying is that the collective mind as understood by Saussure can exist only in present reality, the sum of individual minds. He invokes Freud and Marx to claim that it has a transpresent existence in which exist certain consciousness-determining processes, such as the Oedipus complex and the alienation of man from his species nature. The need for Lévi-Strauss to make such an assertion should be clear from the example I have chosen to illustrate his use of structuralism in anthropology. Saussure, a student of linguistics whose principal research interest was the proto-European language underlying the Aryan tongues, would never have considered examining the possibility of common linguistic structures among Tonga, Trobriand Islanders, and the Cherkess—much less a structural linkage between the languages of these peoples and those of Englishmen and Americans. Lévi-Strauss clearly wishes to seek out and specify universalistic social structures that accordingly must possess both synchronic and diachronic properties. He seeks the structuring of man, while Saussure sought only the structures of languages, distinguishing *la langue*, in which a system exists, from the more general category *langage*, language proper. Lévi-Strauss has assumed that a system exists in *langage*—that is, that a universal language exists as a system.

In performing his analysis of the avunculate, Lévi-Strauss specified dimensions as relations between elements, holding to the Saussurian systems format.[26] He designates these relations as *consanguinity*, *affinity*, and *descent*. Here too he joins Roger Brown, for these relations in turn may be mapped directly to Brown's *lineality*, *sex*, and *generation*. By *affinity* he is designating the sexual relation between spouses, rather than the dimension specifying the gender of the marital pair members. This procedure holds for the other elements of his scheme as well, maintaining a Saussurian emphasis on relations rather than specifying elements. Therefore it is all the more impressive that he arrives at the propositional statement of the avunculate satisfying Brown's geometric representation. From the standpoint of the idea of a system, what is most significant is Lévi-Strauss's attempt to treat social systems as language systems and to do so in a form amenable to treatment with insights drawn from the social theories of Marx, Freud, Mauss, and Durkheim. In his inaugural address, he clearly sees himself as Mauss's successor, as the latter was Durkheim's.[27]

With Lévi-Strauss, action systems are finally reduced to systems of meanings and attitudes. The language system is taken as the system par excellence, since in it, and in it alone, meanings are possible. The organization of the world is based here on the organization of men, as Durkheim and Mauss taught in *Primitive Classification*;[28] and, Lévi-Strauss appears to say, that organization of men is based upon language. In his inaugural address, he wistfully recalls some remarks of Durkheim:

It would not be overbold to suggest that in its oral expression, the teaching of de Saussure must not have been very far from these profound remarks by Durkheim, which, published in 1900, seem to have been written today: "Without a doubt, the phenomena which concern structure are somewhat more stable than functional phenomena, but between the two orders of facts there is only a difference of degree. Structure itself occurs in the process of becoming. . . . It takes shape and breaks down ceaselessly, it is life which has reached a certain degree of consolidation; and to distinguish the life whence it derives from the life it determines would be to dissociate inseparable things."[29]

In our earlier discussion of action systems, we saw that structures and functions are held to be quite distinct from one another. A function is that which is performed by a structure. In the mousetrap system, the structure consists of elements (snare, bait, bar, latch) so organized that each performs one discrete function in the overall system. The system itself also performs a function predicated upon the organization of these elements and functions. In the nonrecursive, cybernetic system, structures reduce to black boxes and functions to relations between outputs and inputs of these boxes. In Parsons' general system of action, this also holds true by virtue of its status as a cybernetic system.[30] All these are systems organized for the control of action.

With the language system we ran into a certain problem. It is an action system, for *parole* is an activity, but it does not lend itself to the same kind of analysis as the other action systems. We saw that this was primarily a consequence of the fact that, although it was a highly complex signaling system, it did not "process' signals but created them as outputs from sets of elements that were themselves only form and whose content came into being only when they occurred as outputs. The peculiar condition resulting from the arbitrary nature of the signifier creates a chaotic amalgam, a matrix of perhaps an infinite number of possible dimensions, upon which human mental activity (what I have chosen to call intentionality) imposes an ordering in the act of articulation. Social psychology furnishes us with some clues as to how this hypothetical matrix is employed by the user, and the results of such research are compatible with the system employed by Lévi-Strauss and the results he obtains.

With Lévi-Strauss and his contemporaries, this system becomes the model for all possible social phenomena. When individuals act or interact with others, they do so in accordance with a model of action based on the same kind of relations as those existing not in the recursive mousetrap or nonrecursive cybernetic systems but in the language system. A vocabulary of action and of organization comes into being.[31] *Function* and *structure* are no longer clearly distinguished in such a system, for as Durkheim is saying in Lévi-Strauss's citation, structure itself occurs in the process of becoming, as it does in language. At the individual level, an actor acts out phrases, sentences, and paragraphs of actions syntagmatically. If these actions are imbued with meaning, in Weber's sense, such meanings exist paradigmatically and therefore are never wholly denotative but subject to a range of interpretation. When we employ *verstehen* and attempt to read the intention of the actor, what we are doing is attempting to read that "line of intentionality" he has "shot through" the paradigmatic clusters of possible actions in his vocabulary. Hence *verstehen* is possible only to the extent that socially oriented activity is a language. Social activity is a form of *parole*, a syntagmatic presentation that excludes other possible acts one could have taken but did not, and its meaning is accordingly derived from what it has excluded.

With language as the system par excellence, with no necessary and sufficient connections to an object world, its mechanisms and rules (and "general laws," as Lévi-Strauss calls them) take precedence in social science above those dictated by otherwise scientific procedures. The ontological status of the natural world is preserved, but epistemology becomes an exercise in grammar. Science is only one form of discourse among many possible forms of discourse, all subject to rules such as those we find governing language, and all discussing not the world of objects and things and events but the relations among the concepts that emerge by virtue of the language we employ.

Notes

1. Ferdinand de Saussure, *The Course in General Linguistics* (New York: McGraw-Hill, 1966), p. 130.

2. See, e.g., his diagram of the French word *enseignment* in Saussure, 1966, p. 126, and *defaire* and *quadrupex* on p. 129.

3. Saussure, 1966, p. 131.

4. Saussure, 1966, pp. 5–6.

5. Saussure, 1966, pp. 15–16.

6. This is discussed more fully in Chapter 7.

7. Saussure, 1966, p. 16n.

8. Charles E. Osgood, George Suci, and P. H. Tannenbaum, *The Measurement of Meaning* (Urbana: University of Illinois Press, 1958).

9. For a concise description, see Delbert C. Miller, *Handbook of Research Design and Social Measurement* 3d. ed. (New York: David McKay, 1977), pp. 95–97.

10. I routinely applied the semantic differential in this way in teaching research methods. At a Jesuit college, I found significant differences in the clustering of the concepts mentioned in the text that were functions of the pre-college backgrounds of the students, dichotomized into parochial and secular secondary school education. The dispersion within and among clusters was consistently much less for those who had attended parochial high schools.

11. However, this does not mean that Saussurian theory is strengthened at the expense of competing theories of language. The semantic differential descends from a body of research that sought initially to reject Saussurian assumptions. See Chapter 7.

12. A. K. Romney and R. D'Andrade, "Cognitive Aspects of English Kin Terms," *American Anthropologist* 66(3), 1964.

13. Roger Brown, *Social Psychology* (New York: Free Press, 1967). See also Roger Brown, *Words and Things* (New York: Free Press, 1968).

14. These are explored in George V. Zito, *The Mask of Agamemnon: Sociological Explorations in Shakespearean Family Structure* (forthcoming).

15. See Chapter 8 for a formal discussion of this matrix.

16. Jacques Derrida, *Of Grammatology* (Baltimore: Johns Hopkins University Press, 1976).

17. Troubetzkoy, Jakobson, and the Prague school continued the Saussurian development of phonology, stressing the sound component of the signifier.

18. Lévi-Strauss, 1963, p. 33.

19. Lévi-Strauss, 1963, p. 41.

20. Lévi-Strauss, 1963, p. 42.

21. Lévi-Strauss, 1963, p. 46.

22. Lévi-Strauss, 1963, p. 42.

23. Lévi-Strauss, 1963, p. 47.

24. Claude Lévi-Strauss, *The Scope of Anthropology* (London: Cape, 1967).

25. Lévi-Strauss, 1967, pp. 28–29.

26. Lévi-Strauss, 1963, p. 46.

27. Lévi-Strauss, 1967, p. 19.

28. Émile Durkheim and Marcel Mauss, *Primitive Classification* (Chicago: University of Chicago Press, 1963). See also David Bloor, "Durkheim and Mauss Revisited: Classification and the Sociology of Knowledge," in J. Law, ed., *The Language of Sociology*, Sociological Review Monographs (Keele, Staffordshire: University of Keele, 1981).

29. Lévi-Strauss, 1967, p. 29.

30. This should be compared with the definitions furnished by Parsons and quoted in Chapter 2.

31. The hypothesis that language shapes our view of reality is not new, nor

is it limited to Saussurian linguistics. The Sapir-Whorf hypothesis is the most familiar form of this assumption. See Benjamin Whorf, *Language, Thought, and Reality* (Cambridge, Mass.: MIT Press, 1956), and Edward Sapir, *Language* (New York: Harcourt Brace, 1921).

The Meaning of "Cause" in Sociology   5

It has been convincingly argued by Simon Clark that Lévi-Strauss's structuralism descends as much from Durkheim and Mauss as it does from Saussure.[1] Clark presents a chronological analysis of the work of Lévi-Strauss and shows how his earlier efforts employ methods and techniques he only later sought to justify in Saussurian terms. However, the issue is more complex than this, for what is true for Lévi-Strauss's work is often true for the work of many of his contemporaries. A tradition has existed within French social thought sufficiently different from that within German or American discourses, and it is this tradition upon which much of what is termed "structuralism" depends. The issue is sufficiently significant to allow us to digress momentarily from our general discussion and consider it briefly.

Ferdinand de Saussure and Émile Durkheim were contemporaries,[2] but there is no biographical evidence to show that they were in any way acquainted with each other or knew of each other's work. Nevertheless, Durkheim was the intellectual giant of his time, particularly to those with interests in the human and social sciences. Many of Saussure's terms, such as *collective mind* and *social fact*, and his overall understanding of the nature of a social collectivity are remarkably close to Durkheim's. In addition, Durkheim and his followers clearly emphasized the synchronic in ways at odds with the kinds of understanding invoked by their German counterparts. The German sociology evolving during Durkheim's lifetime, in particular that of the Weberians, was essentially a study of historical (and therefore of *diachronic*) phenomena. It is a sociology that traces historical processes and seeks causes that might help explain the origins of those social phenomena found in Wilhelmian-Weimar Germany. This sociology was bound to various forms of historicism in ways that French social thought clearly was not. French sociology and social anthropology were directed toward an understanding of collective phenomena as omnipresent "things" in their own right. The positivist tradition in French intellectual thought searched for universal laws; this is emphasized by Saussure and Durkheim and is echoed by Lévi-Strauss in the example he borrowed from Troubetzkoy. Such laws structure the present and regulate the collective conscience. They help explain why things are as they are. In the process of explaining them, recourse is made to empirical data (such as suicide rates and the behavior of Australian aborigines), but only insofar as these serve to illustrate the theoretical assumptions. In French social science, a thing is not "true" simply because empirical data can be found for it. In a sense the French lack the pragmatic-empiricist thrust involved in American social thought. Concrete empirical data are employed by Durkheim and his school only as examples of the thing to be explained, something not appreciated by some misguided latter-day attacks on the methodology of Durkheim's *Suicide*.[3] For the French, anthropology is not an attempt to understand primitive societies for their own sakes. A primitive society is used only as a site for exploration of the conceptual base of the more highly developed Western industrial societies. Durkheim had set the pattern in *The Elementary Forms*. For Weber, on the other hand, the problem was to understand why he found about him a particular mode of commercial activity not present elsewhere. Why is it, he asked, that the Protestant nations of Europe are wealthy and individualized while the Catholic nations are not? He sought the answer not by synchronic analysis but by diachronic analysis. He accordingly employed other cultural groups and other times to search out what they may have lacked that Protestant Europe possessed. The Durkheimians searched for things helping one to understand the operation of the collective mind, how it systematically orders events and attitudes. The idea of a synchronic system is accordingly involved in Durkheimian sociology in a way generally absent from German sociology. A possible exception here is the work of German sociologist Georg Simmel.[4]

Simmel was seen as something of a maverick by his colleagues, a brilliant but erratic and "unsystematic" neo-Kantian. A contemporary of Durkheim and Saussure, Simmel makes many of the distinctions we associate with Saussure. In his essay "How Is Society Possible?" he distinguishes between the synchronic and diachronic.[5] He is less interested in the diachronic analysis characterizing the work of his colleagues. Simmel's synchronic analysis involves an understanding of the social forms that emerge to serve collective human life. It is "life itself" that unfolds these forms, as in the excerpt from Durkheim quoted by Lévi-Strauss in the preceding chapter. These social forms contain oppositions, and it is the relations within these oppositions which make possible particular contents often posed as dialectical contradictions.[6] They are psychological in origin.[7] They make possible many different approaches to our understanding, many different academic disciplines, but no one has priority over others.[8]

Durkheim knew the work of Simmel and thought of it highly enough to translate some into French and subsequently publish it in the *Année Sociologique*. How much of an influence Simmel exerted on the thought of Durkheim is difficult to establish, but it is clear that in Durkheim's later works (particularly in his *Elementary Forms of the Religious Life* and his work with Mauss, *Primitive Classification*) he had moved away considerably from the perspectives expressed in *The Division of Labor in Society* and its Comtean and Saint-Simonian influences and toward the understanding of social processes that characterizes the work of Simmel.

Thus, an intellectual milieu existed on the European continent at the outbreak of the first World War that transcended the nationalistic pride of the French in their attempt to create a "French sociology," independent of anything foreign or German. That a Swiss linguist, a French professor of sociology and education, and a German docent in philosophy who was unable to find an academic slot all contributed to the formation of a "European system of thought"[9] renders the task of separating the origins of the structuralist idea of a system insurmountable.[10]

Hence, Clark's critique of Lévi-Strauss leaves the main problem unresolved. We do not know how much Saussure took from Durkheim nor what Durkheim took from Simmel, nor the reverse of this. What seems clear is that by Lévi-Strauss's time the main principles that were later claimed as structuralist and attributed to Saussure were already the common properties of French social thought and in the process of emerging in various disciplines. This helps explain, among other things, why so many contemporary thinkers classified by their publics as structuralist disclaim the identification.

As we have seen, the peculiar nature of the language system results from the arbitrary nature of the signifier. The individual who employs *parole* is the agency imposing order on a chaotic matrix of possible signifiers. Possibilities of many kinds exist among the relations of the elements of the system. The individual does not create these possibilities; they are collective and not individual products. What the individual does is arrange their possibilities in such a way that they approximate what he means to say, what he intends. He is thus the first cause of that which he articulates, even if that particular sequence of syntagms had been articulated elsewhere and at some other time by someone else. He does not simply parrot sentences he has heard, repeating sets of meanings designating things. He is their author. The content of that which he communicates is an expression of his willful intentions. He is the cause of the *parole* that takes place. He alone is *morally responsible* for what he says.

This whole matter of the role of human agency in the idea of responsibility had been articulated within the *Année* enterprise by Durkheim's student Paul Fauconnet shortly after his mentor's death. Fauconnet tells us in his *La Responsibilité* (published in 1928 and as yet unavailable in English) that Émile Durkheim had treated the whole matter of responsibility in the four lectures of his course on the theory of sanctions, which he gave at Bordeaux in 1894.[11] When he proposed to Durkheim that he write in this area, Durkheim furnished him with the manuscripts of his Bordeaux lectures. Fauconnet claims that he owes his entire education in sociology to Durkheim and that anything of merit in the text is Durkheim's, the errors only being his own. While cautioning us that Durkheim's death and the war prevented his mentor from reading the complete manuscript, he assures us that Marcel Mauss had reviewed the manuscript and made suggestions.

The text is of interest to us here because of its view of agency in social action and, by extension, in *parole*. Here the entire *Année* apparatus of collective conscience, social facts, and collective representations is applied directly to the case of the individual actor.

In any effort to create a scientific sociology, a science of individual actors becomes paramount. Many British and American sociologists, some of whom are less familiar with the *Année* enterprise than their writings lead one to believe, have been excessively critical of the Durkheimians for what they consider their failure to appreciate the part played by the individual actor, claiming that there is an overdeterministic quality to social facts which renders the individual a kind of mousetrap system, free of self-determination. Such a view, which links human phenomena to phenomena of the natural world for its formulation of a science, is rejected by Paul Fauconnet. This is forcefully argued in his discussion of the idea of causality.

Fauconnet argues that there is a causality that is peculiar to man and distinct from that causality we apply in scientific explanations. Natural science knows only secondary causes. Every cause, by itself, is also an effect. Scientific explanation involves one in the tracing of causal chains, where the effect of one cause becomes the cause of a subsequent effect. Also, in the natural sciences concepts such as *cause* and *effect* are the same class of phenomena, things of the same kind, and the laws of scientific causality are intended to describe the necessary relations linking these same kinds of phenomena.

On the other hand, he argues, the person (when we consider him as a cause) is *the first cause*. The act, as Aristotle said, has its beginning in itself. In addition, the two phenomena, actor and action, are heterogeneous. Between them exists not the relation of one phenomenon to another of the same kind, which a scientific law expresses between a cause and effect in the natural sciences, but the relation of producer to product, the workman to the finished work. The actor wills his activity, and the causal chain terminates at him, there being no need to look beyond him for another cause.[12]

Fauconnet was interested in the various applications of the notion of responsibility. Accordingly he finds the actor responsible for his own actions in a causal sense, and explores the implications of this in terms of religious and legal sanctions, an area that does not directly concern us here. Nor need we be concerned with Freudian and Marxist implications of such a perspective. What is of interest is that Fauconnet is treating individual human action (the equivalent of *parole* in an extralinguistic mode of activity) precisely as Saussure treats linguistic activity. The speaker is the first cause of his articulation and the meaning he conveys; the causal chain begins here. The speaker has not been programmed to blurt out certain redundant sentences, nor has the actor been programmed to enact fixed sets of activities. These are constructed by the intentional agency of the speaker/actor from the sets of paradigmatic and syntagmatic possibilities his collectivity has furnished him. "The act is mine, and mine alone," Fauconnet tells us. Similarly, the sentence I write is mine, and mine alone. The laws of libel and of plagiarism are sanctions imposed upon the author of words meaningfully associated, as the laws of equity and torts impose sanctions for certain nonverbal activities.

Fauconnet's view of the operation of social facts is identical to that of Saussure's. The social facts of language are not mere stimuli invoking fixed tropistic responses, and neither are the social facts of the social system as envisioned by Durkheim's *Année* school. Social facts of whatever kind are possibilities in a grammar of possible acts. If men do indeed possess a "rhetoric of motives," in Kenneth Burke's sense, they are not essential to the system of possible meanings involved in the idea of a system in structuralist thought; they are sets of contingent syntagms that redundantly prove useful in explaining, or explaining away, intentional, human activity.

Max Weber tells us, in what is now included as the "Author's Preface" in the English edition of *The Protestant Ethic and the Spirit of Capitalism* that he was interested in determining the operations in the causal chain leading to the emergence of a distinctive form of rational capitalism in the West. Elsewhere Weber emphasizes the importance of considering the human actor as the agency of all social processes. Things do not happen because of institutionalized and bureaucratic patterns of organization; they happen because individual actors perform specific ideographic acts. How such acts lead to the causal chains of the type sought is left unexplained by the Weberians. In the present context it is important to note that this kind of causal chain is dismissed by the *Année* school. Human actors are the cause of their activity, and no recourse to causal chains is necessary. Durkheim discusses the etiology of suicide in terms of its sources, the groups within which suicides are likely to occur, not in terms of naturalistic scientific causes; there are French Protestants who do not commit suicide, bachelors who do not, Roman Catholics who do.[13] The laws sought by Durkheim and his methodological heirs (and here we must include Lévi-Strauss) are not of the kind found in the natural sciences but are mentalistic or moral laws specifying *what ought to be* taken into account, not *what is* taken into account—that is, what syntagmatic orderings are preferable from the standpoint of the collective conscience, namely, what is specified as normative and hence not subject to sanctions by the collectivity. The individual is not denied the possibility of constructing possible courses of action. He is the exercisor of his own free will and is accordingly accountable for his actions.

Thus, the theoretical schema at the level of social action was worked out by Durkheim and his students as a synchronic system, lacking only the connection to language which Saussure was able to furnish. Once the meaning of the *Course* became evident, it could be employed, as Lévi-Strauss and others have employed it, to help explain the kind of synchronic system the Durkheimians had articulated.

Although the transcendental neo-Kantian biases of structuralism as we have been discussing it are evident throughout, its implied rejection of the application of philosophical strictures to its methods of analysis arises exclusively from its concern with language as *the* paradigm par excellence rather than rationality as the paradigm. Here too it is anti-Weberian, anti-German. Philosophy is reduced to one more mode of discourse, no more and no less logically prior in specifying rules of explanation than other modes. Indeed, philosophy is seen as subservient to language and therefore lost in a pointless search for that which it cannot possibly attain. As the language system is understood here, the notion of a metaphysical essence is dispensed with, and so too is the notion of causality as it is known in the natural sciences. Weber's ideal types, performed by exaggerating the individual characterizing properties of some social phenomenon, become frozen, fixed syntagms attempting somehow to provide a definitive encoding of meaning where such definition is not possible so long as words are the signifiers. Ideal types are logocentric. For structuralism generally, there can be no *geist*, diachronically working out its teleological purpose in human history. In the structuralist version of the gospel, in the beginning there was not "the word"; there was only the act that made the word possible, that articulated it and in doing so gave it meaning.

Notes

1. See note 8, Chapter 1.

2. Saussure taught somewhat earlier than Durkheim in Paris at the École Pratique des Hautes Études from 1880 to 1891. At Paris he taught Sanskrit, Gothic, and Old High German. In 1891 he accepted a professorship at the University of Geneva. Not until 1906 did he begin teaching general linguis-

tics. He died in 1912, the year Durkheim published *The Elementary Forms of the Religious Life*. Durkheim died in 1917.

3. George V. Zito, "Durkheimian Suicides in Shakespeare," *Omega* 4(4), 1973.

4. And yet, according to his critics, Simmel did not produce a systematic sociology. In light of what we have uncovered about the semiotic system, however, this matter requires further investigation. Simmel has influenced American sociology more than any other classical theorist, largely through the efforts of the Chicago school. Albion Small, Robert Park, and Nicholas Spykman had all attended Simmel's lectures in Berlin. Some of these influences have been traced by Donald Levine in two consecutive papers, "Simmel's Influence on American Sociology," *American Journal of Sociology* 81 (3 and 4), 1976. Simmel's influence on Max Weber is well known.

5. Georg Simmel, "How Is Society Possible?" in Donald N. Levine, ed., *Georg Simmel on Individuality and Social Forms* (Chicago: University of Chicago Press, 1971), p. 16.

6. Simmel, in Levine, 1971, p. 13.

7. Simmel, in Levine, 1971, p. 34.

8. Nicholas J. Spykman, *The Social Theory of Georg Simmel* (New York: Atherton, 1966).

9. Peter Lawrence, *Georg Simmel, Sociologist and European* (New York: Barnes & Noble, 1976).

10. Significantly, Parsons places the willful, intentional actor *within* the system and Saussure places the willful intentionality of the actor *outside* the system, but for Simmel "A society is, therefore, a structure which consists of beings who stand inside and outside of it at the same time" (Simmel, "How Is Society Possible?" in Levine, 1971, p. 15).

11. Paul Fauconnet, *La Responsibilité* (Paris: Alcan, 1928).

12. This was appreciated by Fritz Heider in his formulation of what became known as "Attribution Theory." See George V. Zito and Jerry Jacobs, "Attribution and Symbolic Interaction: An Impasse at the Generalized Other," *Human Relations* 32(7), 1979. It is significant that attribution theory finds itself at odds with symbolic interactionism. Herbert Blumer's symbolic interactionism owes its genesis to Charles Morris's compilation on notes of Mead's lectures, which Morris published as *Mind, Self, and Society* (1934) much as Bally and Sechehay published their notes on Saussure's lectures as *Cours in linguistique generale* (1916); *The Course in General Linguistics*). In Chapter 7 we see that Morris later aligned himself with a school of semiology extremely critical of Saussure. In Lévi-Strauss's terms, Morris is to Mead what Bally and Sechehay are to Saussure. The differences in the two theories of language have had unintentional consequences, for if I am correct in seeing Lévi-Strauss's heavy dependence on the Durkheimians, it was inevitable that a theory of social psychology seeking to incorporate Fauconnet's idea of cau-

sality should at last collide with another theory of social psychology based upon Blumer's understanding of Morris's understanding of Mead. This is not idle speculation; it relates directly to the idea of discourse championed by Michel Foucault and discussed in Chapter 6.

13. Émile Durkheim, *Suicide* (New York: Free Press, 1951).

Structures and Discourses: From Lévi-Strauss to Foucault   6

If the idea of a system in structuralist thought liberates the social sciences from concerns that have directed as well as constricted its development, it liberates them into a state of causal and essential anarchy. It allows alternative patterns to be applied to historical phenomena with little regard for those ''facts'' that may have previously dominated the reconstruction of an event or happening. Again, an illustration from Lévi-Strauss is appropriate.

We have already seen that Lévi-Strauss wished to transcend Saussure's critical distinction between *parole* and *la langue* so as to include Freudian and Marxist understandings of collective phenomena. In his *Structural Anthropology* he treats the Oedipus myth as a system of semiotic signs that disclose an unexpected relation.[1]

The story of Oedipus, as contained in the Sophocles plays and elsewhere, is a kind of narrative account of events with some flashbacks to earlier details of the story told by the chorus, Terisias and Oedipus. The flashbacks are part of an integrated narrative; however, one could, if he chose, tell the Oedipus story wholly syntagmatically: the child was born, the parents warned, the child abandoned; grown to manhood, the child unknowingly slays his father, confronts the Sphinx, marries his mother, and so on. Word event follows word event, syntagm follows syntagm.

Lévi-Strauss does something quite different. He arranges the Oedipus narrative syntagmatically, as in a sentence moving from left to right, in the form ''Oedipus kills his father, Laios; Oedipus kills the Sphinx,

Oedipus marries his mother. . . . ,'' where event follows on event in the same sequence as the narrative, but he locates them in a matrix that discloses certain common features of the narrative. This matrix is composed of four columns and as many horizontal rows as are necessary to complete the narrative sequence (see Figure 6.1).

The first three columns in Figure 6.1 are read from left to right until the line ends; then one drops down to the next row and continues reading, and so on. Reading the figure in this way, the syntagmatic content narrates the events in the myth as follows: Cadmos seeks his sister Europa, ravished by Zeus; he then kills the dragon. The Spartoi kill one another. Then Oedipus kills his father, Laios, then he kills the Sphinx, then he marries his mother, Jocasta. His son Eteocles then kills his brother Polynices. At the end, Antigone (Oedipus' daughter) buries her brother Polynices despite the prohibition announced by Creon (Oedipus' successor) against burying the body.

Consider, however, the common features of the items included in each column. Each column contains a bundle of significant paradigmatic relations. The operation Lévi-Strauss is performing is similar to

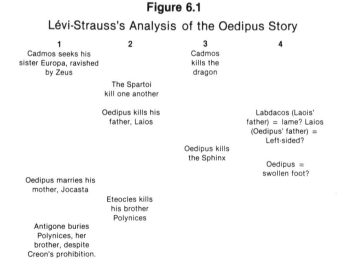

Figure 6.1

Lévi-Strauss's Analysis of the Oedipus Story

1	2	3	4
Cadmos seeks his sister Europa, ravished by Zeus		Cadmos kills the dragon	
	The Spartoi kill one another		
	Oedipus kills his father, Laios		Labdacos (Laois' father) = lame? Laios (Oedipus' father) = Left-sided?
		Oedipus kills the Sphinx	
			Oedipus = swollen foot?
Oedipus marries his mother, Jocasta			
	Eteocles kills his brother Polynices		
Antigone buries Polynices, her brother, despite Creon's prohibition.			

that shown in Figure 4.1, where we considered the Saussurian analysis of the syntagm *mis-fit*.

Examining the bundle of significant relations in the first column of Figure 6.1, Lévi-Strauss suggests that they specify an overrating of blood relations, while the second column specifies an underrating of blood relations. The third column, he states, represents a kind of denial of the autochthonous origin of man, since in both cases included in this column a man is shown killing a monster that is born of earth in order for man to live. The fourth column is not a part of the narrative sequence. What is here signified is a system of significant relations within the names used in the myth. The names are those of grandfather, father, and son. These are seen by Lévi-Strauss as associated with the persistence of the idea of man's autochthonous origin, since it is a theme in mythology that men born of the earth cannot walk properly at first.

Lévi-Strauss concludes that the Oedipus myth represents an attempt to reconcile two conflicting views of man's origin. One mythological view holds that man is born of the earth itself,[2] but the other recognizes that men descend from other men and women. The Oedipus story, Lévi-Strauss believes, is an attempt to solve this contradiction by equating the two, the blood relation and the earth relation. This is indicated by the two sets of contradictions in Figure 6.1: the contradiction between columns 1 and 2 and that between columns 3 and 4. Both pairs of relations are included in the myth, and the acceptance of both pairs meaningfully associated together is what the myth accomplishes. "By a correlation of this type," Lévi-Strauss assures us, "the overrating of blood relations is to the under-rating of blood relations as the attempts to escape autochthony is to the impossibility to succeed."[3]

While many objections may be raised to the "explanation" Lévi-Strauss furnishes here, and I shall raise some shortly, what is interesting about it is the method he employs, separating possible paradigmatic relations from syntagmatic relations without destroying the sequence of the latter, and then finding other proportionalities among the isolated syntagms.

While the method is clearly derivable from the *Course*, however, the possibilities it unleashes can be ordered only by the intentionality of the analyst. This places the whole matter beyond the realm of scientific proof. No hypothesis is here falsifiable, in Popper's sense. The analyst, employing his own creative intuition and his knowledge of similar myths, only infers that particular meaning or set of meanings he finally obtains. This is a hermeneutic operation. If the process involved in employing a language system is as described in the previous chapter, then it is clear that speakers may say many things at once while employing a single set of possible signifiers. This is what Cassandra does, or Terisias does, or Nostradamus, or the Delphic Oracle. One can speak in such a way that what is communicated depends upon the decoding performed by the listener, who must shoot his own line of intentionality through the sequence of signifiers one has furnished him with in speaking. Myth often has this quality about it. What Lévi-Strauss is saying is that the Oedipus myth has this quality about it; it is an inchoate attempt to resolve the contradiction between man being born of earth and man being born of woman, a contradiction that may not be resolved. Oedipus, the club-footed one who bears the stigma of his earth birth, goes back into the body of Jocasta who bore him, and she bears him his brothers Eteocles and Polynices and his sister Antigone. His children are his siblings, at least maternally. Jocasta becomes the primeval earth-mother, giving us birth, and all men are accordingly brothers. Here I am exploring Lévi-Strauss's interpretation of the myth, employing my own intuition. But what I have said here is mine alone. There are no criteria for determining the "validity" of my extension of Lévi-Strauss's interpretation, as there are none for determining the validity of his. An appeal to the text will not help either of us, for here the interpretation is open, not closed. The system can produce a plethora of meanings from the same cryptic mythological utterance. If this were not so, the Delphic Oracle's pronouncements would be subject to the same rules of truth and falseness as the *polis* applied in everyday life.

Further objections may be made to Lévi-Strauss's interpretation. If we consider the entries made in the columns of Figure 6.1, we see that it is the analyst's choice which column is selected for a particular event. The only requirement is that the events form a narrative sequence. In addition, it is the analyst who selects which events are to be included in the matrix and which are to be eliminated. We see no inclusion in the matrix of certain memorable events of the myth, such as the warnings of Terisias, or Oedipus tearing out his eyes, or Antigone volunteering to act as her blind father's guide. The reply can be made that these details do not point to the set of unconscious relations that nonetheless exist in the myth and are here revealed. However, the inclusion of the nonnarrative column 4 clearly challenges this reply.

Column 4 has been added by the analyst and has to do with possible meaning contents in the names of the male characters who descend from one another. They all seem to be lame. Nothing about autochthony is directly stated. That lameness and autochthony are sometimes associated does not arise from analysis of the text itself, but is an external bit of evidence that Lévi-Strauss introduces to make sense out of the myth. This fourth column, then, does not have the same relation to the text as the other three columns, which belong to a highly selective reading of the story line. But Lévi-Strauss does not take this untoward relation into account, and treats column 4 as if it had the same epistemic relation to the myth as the other three.

If we examine the matrix as Lévi-Strauss has arranged it and ignore this intrusive fourth column, other sets of meanings spring at once to mind. What I find in the first entry of the first column is a rape; the second entry of the first column is incest; the first entry of the second column is murder, its second entry patricide, its third entry fratricide. I can therefore construct a matrix coterminous with that constructed by Lévi-Strauss, but omitting his nontextual fourth column, which has the appearance of Figure 6.2.

Figure 6.2

Another Analysis of the Oedipus Story

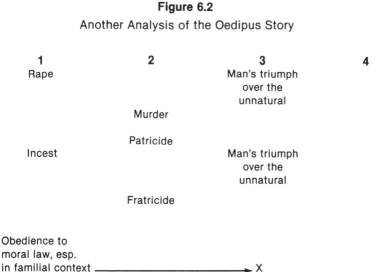

The last and final entry, involving Antigone's actions, I would assign to the bottom of column 3, rather than the bottom of column 1, where Lévi-Strauss has placed it. Without doing violence to his new method, we can then collapse these three columns into two:

1	2
Rape	Man's triumph over the unnatural
Murder	
Patricide	Man's triumph over the unnatural
Incest	
fratricide	Obedience to moral law, esp. in familial context

We see that column 1 enumerates negatively sanctioned behaviors, while column 2 enumerates positively sanctioned behaviors. What the myth is saying is that man has the capacity to triumph over the unnatural as well as succumb to it; his nature is dualistic, a set of mutual oppositions. This is not only in keeping with the details of the Oedipus myth and with Lévi-Strauss's method, but also with Western thought generally. In Christian mythology, for example, it finds expression in St. Paul's "I know the law and I see it, but I find another law in my members, at war with the law of my mind," which is echoed by St. Augustine in his *Confessions* and St. Thomas Aquinas in the *Summa Theologica*. It was the problem addressed by the Manichaeans and the Zoroastrians also. In short, it can be shown, by the same set of elements selected by Lévi-Strauss and by the same method as he employs, that the Oedipus myth when subjected to structural analysis reveals what it has always been taken to reveal: a moral injunction against "unnatural" social behavior and a recognition of the difficulty of obeying the injunction.

When I, a sociologist, compare the last figure with that supplied by Lévi-Strauss (Fig. 6.1), my interpretation seems to me more parsimonious and more direct, more "scientific." To be sure, Oedipus has something "unnatural" about him in his club-footedness. But this biological stigma becomes insignificant in light of the social stigma that accrues from murdering one's father and sexually coupling with one's mother. This, it seems to me, is what the Oedipus story is all about.

However, as soon as I make this statement it must be clear that there is nothing truly definitive that may be said about the Oedipus story. If it contains some measure of universality in meaning, that meaning, by the rules of this system, is what I infer, or you infer, or Lévi-Strauss infers from imposing intentional mental operations on the syntagmatic and paradigmatic possibilities it specifies. The meaning does not lie in the thing itself. It is not possible, on the basis of the system we defined in the last few chapters, that the Oedipus story could have some incontestable *essential* meaning. The words we have in the Oedipus plays belong to Sophocles, and to him alone, at least in this form. Although their possibilities were furnished to him by Athenian society, he alone, in Fauconnet's terms, is responsible for his creation. If Freud or Lévi-Strauss or myself find *additional* possibilities in the narrative, then we must recognize these as creations of Freud or Lévi-Strauss or myself. In much the same way, the reader may find meanings other than those found by Freud, Lévi-Strauss, or the writer. We may argue among ourselves about which interpretation is the best one and perhaps agree, but even this agreement is another phenomenon taking place at the level of language, or what we should more properly refer to as the level of *discourse*, and has no relation to anything but itself.

If we take one small step backward, we see that what is involved in the specification of unintended consequences[4] or latent functions is the discovery of a variation in a syntagmatic discourse that we could not have anticipated. A different way of discussing an event or events results because of the possibilities in language which we could not have foreseen on the basis of our own discourse. Indeed, this is precisely what occurs in Merton's example of the bank failure in his discussion of W. I. Thomas's *definition of the situation* and *self-fulfilling prophecy*.[5] When a different and unexpected way of talking about a possible event occurs, the results conform to this different way of talking, that is, they lend themselves to explanation in this mode of discourse. Definitions of situations are linguistic procedures, the specification of particular signs. Similarly, system maintenance, in the sense employed by Parsons as an internal concern of the system,[6] involves imposing restrictions on discourse to ensure a high measure of predictability in system performance. This means minimizing the possibility of latent functions that may be dysfunctional to the maintenance of the discourse. This helps explain why Marx was slighted by the Parsonians in their explication of social theory: Marxist ideas are dysfunctional to the idea of a system proposed by Parsons, as is any form of conflict.

There are in language manifest functions of high predictability; the operators *and, or, but, if,* and so forth are signifiers encoding manifest functions. But other signifiers are so rich in possible meanings that innumerable unanticipated consequences occur, allowing us to arrive at verbal formulations that surprise us. The belief that some are positively dysfunctional for the system (such as those involved in the signifiers *rape, fratricide, incest,* and so on) is highly salient in most moral and legal discourses.

All the above are representative of the essential and causal anarchy into which the idea of a system in structuralist thought may lead us. It allows us to treat all other systems, and by implication all previous systems of thought, as discourses exploring the processes in language. This need not be taken as an iconoclastic attack on serious scholarship, although that may be one of the consequences. It appears instead to move the social sciences beyond their present impasse by opening up the whole matter of what it is we mean by an understanding of social phenomena. If, as Karl Mannheim suggested, there are ideological monopolizations of our collective social reality, we are given clues to understanding and methods of examining them. In addition, we are liberated from conventional scientistic constraints that ape the natural sciences although unable to attain their certainty. So long as our discourse seems to make sense to others, it may be as legitimate *as a discourse* as the popular or inherited ones. The arbitrary nature of the signifier guarantees this.

Michel Foucault has taken up this possibility and attempts to carry it through, particularly with regard to the history of ideas and the "epistemes" associated with them.[7] If Lévi-Strauss is the "father of structuralism" in the social sciences, then Foucault, the heir apparent, closes out the movement before moving on to other things. His program and method are set forth in "The Discourse on Language," included as an appendix in the English-language edition of *The Archaeology of Knowledge*. According to Colin Gordon, author of the "Afterword" in Foucault's book of essays on power, "it is sometimes supposed that Foucault's subsequent thematization of power jettisons as obsolete the ambitious edifice of the *Archaeology*. In fact, the features of the latter . . . form the essential ground for the further concepts Foucault was to introduce."[8] This is an apparent rebuttal of those who claim Foucault abandoned his earlier methods. Although Foucault had disclaimed the structuralist label, it is clear that his is a predictable development of applying Saussurian methods to the history of ideas or, more properly, to the history of discourses. Foucault moved beyond Lévi-Strauss with a program based on certain admittedly revolutionary premises. His major concern is not the structure among signs that so interested the latter, but those extended syntagms such as institutionalized discourses and the constraints and relations governing their production.

The "Discourse on Language" was a lecture delivered at the College of France in 1970. Like Mannheim, Foucault recognizes that "In every society the production of discourse is at once controlled, selected, organized and redistributed according to a certain number of procedures, whose role is to avert its powers and its dangers, to cope with chance events, to evade its ponderous, awesome materiality."[9] I have already suggested what some of these procedures are. An author is granted a certain binding authority to his intended meaning; this is legitimated by academic credentials, professional associations, and the division of knowledge within the academy. Each discipline involves at least one or more discourses, and only those qualified by some socially institutionalized agency may engage in such discourse and be taken seriously. The territory assigned to these disciplines is zealously guarded by its trustees, and efforts of related disciplines to encroach upon it are fought off. Power relations may not be neglected in any analytical treatment of such discourse. The power dimension has attained increasing importance in Foucault's recent work. Since discourses tend to overlap, the academic "turf" becomes a battleground for the right to speak with authority.

A sociologist and a cultural anthropologist may find different meanings within the same data set as a result of the differing assumptions governing their fields. This is clear in my interpretation of Lévi-Strauss's Oedipus data. Of course, a colleague of mine may arrive at some other set of meanings, but it will probably be closer to mine than to Lévi-Strauss's if he and I are both sociologists. I will listen closely to what he has to say so long as he is able to legitimate his interpretation by means of sociological premises I recognize. On the other hand, if someone else interprets these data, I will pay little attention to the interpretation unless he has some kind of credentials I recognize. In addition, most people will pay more attention to what Lévi-Strauss says, or even to what I say, than to what non-social scientists may say about so-called "primitive peoples." In the United States, where psychological discourses exercise broad power, the Freudian Oedipus will meet with more acceptance than either of the above.

Thus, any discourse is limited in a number of different ways. Some of these, Foucault argues, are wholly external to the discourse itself.[10] These external constraints operate principally to limit the individual's expression of power and desire, things we feel uncomfortable about hearing expressed. The constraints include such things as prohibited words, which we may not say in our discourse or utter publicly. Two other such external constraints limiting expressions of power and desire he refers to as "the division of madness" and "the will to truth." The former labels certain ways of speaking as madness, although what constitutes madness has varied diachronically and is always subject to negotiation or legal test. A mad person of the medieval period was considered a fool, but such folly was seen to possess a certain therapeutic power on the hearer, as it had among the ancient Greeks or among the Hebrews at the time of the prophets. In Shakespeare's plays the words of fools and madmen are fecund with meaning. In accepting his fool's madness, Lear realizes his own humanity; when mad Ophelia speaks, we read another kind of order into what she says and see beyond what her fellow characters are allowed to see. When Jacques, in *As You Like It*, meets a fool in the forest, the fool's words are recounted with affection and a sense of appreciation of their playful wisdom.

But when Freud turned his attention to the words of his patients, he made sense of them not in terms of their discourse but in terms of his own, treating them as pathological signs of something else. A mad person became not merely foolish but sick. Jacques Laçan, a structuralist psychoanalyst, has tried listening to the discourse itself, making sense in its terms rather than his own. We have erected barricades against such discourses, because they threaten the kind of stability and order in discourse we prefer to have about us. Foucault sees us as victims of the logophobia of the West, a fear of hearing anything in discourse that is spontaneous or vital; we find it threatening and unnerving because it pushes us toward the existential brink of dangerous possibilities. This, he believes, lurks behind our professed logophilia.

Institutional structures such as universities are ways of ordering collective discourse, of making it safe by defusing its intrinsic possibilities. Also, middle-class American speech is especially typical of this. Although it is characterized by an expanded vocabulary, it is stripped of vigor, passion, and authenticity. It reproduces speech patterns that lack the evocative imagery of working-class language.[11] In recent years social scientists such as R. D. Laing, Christopher Lasch, Clifford Geertz, and Richard Sennett have all sought to challenge such castrated middle-class speech, but on very guarded terms and with only limited success. In semiotics, structuralists such as Roland Barthes attempted the same sort of thing.[12]

The third variety of prohibitions operating externally is what Foucault refers to as "the will to truth." Here he connects directly with Nietzsche's perspective. Something designated as *truth* is claimed to have an essential, absolute existence and by searching is held to be attainable; indeed, some aspects of it are supposedly already attained. One cannot challenge the ideological monopolizations of social reality and be allowed to function successfully in his society. At worst, he is branded as mad by his colleagues, as Nietzsche was when he showed how Christianity had reversed the natural order by extolling the weak and deprecating the strong. This "will to truth" is a perverse form of the will and has come to dominate all other external forms of constraint, so that the division of madness and word prohibitions all tend to reinforce it and lose ground to it.[13] These are Durkheimian social facts of high coercive power.

Foucault also finds three internal sets of constraints on discourse. The first of these he calls "commentary." These are the traditional texts vested with high authority (Homer, Dante, Shakespeare, the Bible, Blackstone, and so on) that continue to exert their influences by repetition and reiteration (Joyce restates the *Odyssey*, the King James Bible restates Tyndale, the New Standard Revised Version of the Bible restates the King James Bible, and so on). Often the author's identity continues to exert a measure of control over what is restated, although as we saw with Lévi-Strauss's analysis of the Oedipus myth or with Freud's this becomes compromised. Commentary exists in literary, scientific, juridical, and religious texts and asserts its authority and that of its authors) by its venerability.

The academic disciplines, the second of these sets of constraints, are opposed to commentary, even as they are forced to teach it. They seek to issue new statements, legitimating later author identities, and to fix the conditions under which this may take place.[14]

The third and last internal constraint is associated with the ''qualifications'' (shaman, professor, witch doctor) to speak. Only the ordained may employ the ritualistic speech of their discourse and expect to be taken seriously.

The three sets of constraints internal to discourse tend to limit *events* and the *operation of chance*, as the three external sets limited *desire* and *power*. These are shown in Table 6.1.

Table 6.1
Constraints on Discourse

EXTERNAL	INTERNAL
Limit Power, Desire	*Limit Events, Chance*
1. Prohibited words	Commentary
2. Division of madness	Disciplines
3. The will to truth	Qualifications

All categories of constraints shown in Table 6.1 operate together as consequences and collective representations of the logophobia of the West, its fears of unfettered discourse. Recalling Saussure, these constraints all operate by exclusion; what has been selected out of the wide range of paradigmatic possibilities has eliminated alternative possibilities. Accordingly, discourses develop into orthodoxies with institutional supports, and what is proscribed gives the orthodoxy its meaning. To analyze rather than efface this logophobia,[15] Foucault calls upon us to accept three prescriptions we otherwise would tend to resist.

1. Question the "will to truth."
2. Restore to discourse its character as an event.
3. Abolish the sovereignty of the signifier.

The last of these does not mean the Saussurian signifier, but the author, the identity, the legitimated speaker, the original source—he who signifies. From this perspective it makes little difference which interpretation of the Oedipus myth is mine or Lévi-Strauss's or Freud's. Fauconnet is correct, of course; the act, verbal or otherwise, is mine alone. But it is the discourse, not the speaker, which Foucault seeks to make central. The text, and it alone, is what constitutes the material of discourse, not the speaker. This approach brings about certain methodological demands.

1. *Employ the principle of reversal.* This involves recognizing the negative or exclusionary aspects of those elements in a discourse which at first glance seem to perform positive functions. This dialectical emphasis appears to have been acquired by Foucault from his mentor, Jean Hypolite, whom he salutes as emotionally in the "Discourse" as Lévi-Strauss saluted Mauss in his own inaugural address, cited previously. In the history of discourses, this procedure could profit from Simmel's use of oppositions.

2. *Employ the principle of discontinuity.* This involves seeing discourse as noncontinuous, although at times its elements may chance to fall together. "It is clearly no longer possible to establish mechanically causal links, or an ideal necessity among their constitutive elements. We must accept the introduction of chance as a category in the production of events."[16] In other words, we must recognize that our usual attempts at imposing syntagmatic patterns on events may be in error; an imposed linearity in sequencing masks the operation of the part played by randomness in historical events. This reiterates the anticausal thrust we found to characterize the structuralist idea of a system. Foucault especially dismisses the notion of a causal or teleological *geist*: "History has long since abandoned its attempts to understand events in terms of cause and effect in the formless unity of some great evolutionary process whether vaguely homogeneous or rigidly hierarchised."[17]

3. *Employ the principle of specificity.* See discourse as "a violence we do to things," a practice we impose on them that alters them. It is

this act of imposing linear syntagmatic order that gives the events of discourse their regularity, not anything in the things themselves.

4. *Employ the principle of exteriority.* Instead of trying to burrow to the heart of some event, look to the external conditions comprising its environment and fixing its limits. This is similar to an approach taken by the early Georg Lukács.[18] We need not be enslaved to a view that considers all political and economic phenomena as responses to the material conditions of a particular epoch or the manifestation of some unconscious libidinal life-force. Coupled with the principle of discontinuity, we can search for the accidental disjunctions that commentators have glossed over in their attempts to impose a rational linear order that may not have existed, or an order predicated on the syntagmatic continuity of their a priori assumptions about what should have happened.

Similarly, it may not make much sense to consider, as we did before, whether Saussure knew Durkheim's work, and so on; this question only arises because of a bias in the history of ideas that credits the signifier with sovereignty over the words he has written or uttered; these may not belong to him properly but may be the communal property of the language group within which the discourse takes place. The discourse has a life of its own, collectively molded but not necessarily purposively shaped to some end.

Foucault ends his discourse with a rhetorical flourish: ''And now let those who are weak on vocabulary, let those with little comprehension of theory call all this—if its appeal is stronger than its meaning for them—structuralism.''[19]

Within the definition offered in Chapter 1, we have no problem calling this structuralism, although Foucault has advanced its initial program. Looking back at Lévi-Strauss's analysis of the Oedipus myth, we see that the latter has employed similar, although not identical, techniques.

1. *Reversal.* Lévi-Strauss employs Foucault's *reversal* when he contrasts earth origin and woman origin, the overrating of blood relations and the underrating of such relations, the need to explain origins and the impossibility of such explanation. ''This involves recognizing the negative or exclusionary aspects of those elements which, at first sight, appear to perform positive functions,'' as stated in Foucault's definition.

2. *Discontinuity.* The elements Lévi-Strauss selects from the narra-

tive are taken out of their syntagmatic relationship by being placed in columns that form a discontinuous series.

3. *Specificity*. In destroying the order of the narrative, it comes to mean, for him, something other than what Sophocles understood it to mean or what it has come to mean from the commentary of other authors, notably Sigmund Freud. Lévi-Strauss thus destroys the sovereignty of the signifier.

4. *Exteriority*. Lévi-Strauss does not explore all possibilities, but looks to the external conditions within which the myth arose. The myth is taken to be an expression not of itself but of something else, an unconscious and irrational effort to explain a basic contradiction in our understanding of our origins.

These principles may also be applied to Lévi-Strauss's discussion of the avunculate, discussed in Chapter 5. Thus, Lévi-Strauss's structuralism appears to presuppose many of Foucault's seemingly radical propositions. However, it is clear that Lévi-Strauss does not focus on *discourse*; what Foucault has done is adapt certain aspects of structuralism to a much broader problem—the problem of knowledge itself and its intersection with language. His project is more ambitious than that of the earlier structuralists, and he continuously modifies it as he works through it. Indeed, he is himself part and parcel of the problem he attempts to understand, as he is himself engaged in a discourse, however discontinuous its presentation in the publications he has authored.

In his analysis, Lévi-Strauss attempts to restore to discourse its character as an event. His interpretations are startling, innovative, unexpected. As an academic, he is "opposed to commentary," and the Oedipus myth is just such an authoritative text commentators expound upon. It is a venerable text. It continues to exert its influence and is reiterated and reinterpreted redundantly. But as an academic, Lévi-Strauss has a hidden desire to pursue his will to truth. He believes he has found the "true" meaning of the Oedipus myth. However, analysis of his data shows that there are other more likely interpretations. Our attempt to order this discourse does less violence to the signs he uncovers, and hence its specificity is more limited than his. In our use of discontinuity, exteriority, and reversal, however, we are close to his own. Exteriority suffers somewhat in the alternative explanation, for what we find is an extended expression of the normative obligations that we always tend to find in traditional materials. We fail to restore to discourse its character as an event for this reason. My judgment has probably been influenced by my external knowledge of the conditions under which Greek ritual tragedy arose and the function it performed in providing a catharsis of the audience.

Foucault appears to be employing techniques that are the implicit property of structuralist anthropology and of the French structuralist discourse generally, although to another end. His idea of a system does not deviate from what we have uncovered in Chapter 3. We have little difficulty applying the structuralist label to him, at least at this stage of his career. His later concerns with power and knowledge stem directly from these earlier concerns. His program is a concern with linguistic signs at the level of the highly extended syntagm, the discourse, which has certain diachronic features as well. He cites Saussure[20] and has more than a passing familiarity with the work of his contemporary structuralists. Since Foucault, like Lévi-Strauss, is the heir to a long tradition in French thought treating of collective representations and classificatory operations, he may have arrived at his present epistemological position independently of Saussure's rediscovery, but this is also true of Lévi-Strauss and much of the movement generally. As one of the many intellectual heirs of Durkheim, Mauss, and the *Année Sociologique*, he connects with structuralism, as does Lévi-Strauss, primarily in that his is a concern with *language as a social fact*, with all the coercive power that Durkheimian notion involves. This is the key to his notion of power. He has the same disdain of causality and essence as the other Saussurians, and for many of the same reasons. He brings to their discourse a strong background in philosophy, psychology, and history. These are disciplines that treat the problems of ideas and meanings in diverse ways. If the linguistic sign links an idea with a sound image in the arbitrary relation that Saussure specified, and if by discourse we understand an extended syntagmatic sequence of events, verbal or otherwise, then it is precisely to this order of things that Foucault addresses himself, whether it is the emergence of prisons and mental hospitals, our strange preoccupation with our sexuality, or the prior existence of the ships of fools.

With a social science program such as that begun by Lévi-Strauss and expanded upon by Michel Foucault, the idea of progress disappears. There are only random events that we may link together in innumerable ways, irrespective of anterior or posterior events with which our causal bias urges us to unite them. History holds no intrinsic, progressive pattern, despite the irreversibility of time or entropy. What this agenda seems to call for is a kind of *Finnegans Wake* of the social sciences, where notions float into collective consciousness, are mutated according to certain principles, and then disappear as randomly as they came. "History," Joyce wrote, "is the nightmare from which I am trying to awake." In the program of Michel Foucault, the desperate attempt to awaken is finally abandoned.

Notes

1. Claude Lévi-Strauss, *Structural Anthropology* (New York: Basic Books, 1963), pp. 213–19.

2. The autochthony theme is also present in the Old Testament, where there are two different versions of creation. In Gen. 2:7, man is created out of the dust of the ground, but in Gen. 1:26–27 man and woman are created simultaneously in God's own image.

3. Lévi-Strauss, 1963, p. 216.

4. The distinction between manifest and latent functions in Mertonian functionalism involves the presence or absence of intentionality in the consequences of the action.

5. Robert K. Merton, *Social Theory and Social Structure* (New York: Free Press, 1957), pp. 421ff.

6. See Chapter 2.

7. See, e.g., Michel Foucault, *The Archaeology of Knowledge* (New York: Harper & Row, 1976), and the references cited in note 3 of Chapter 1 of this book. For an attempt to understand Foucault's goals, see Edith Kurzweil, "Michel Foucault: Ending the Era of Man," *Theory and Society* 4(3), 1977, and her *The Age of Structuralism* (New York: Columbia University Press, 1980).

8. Michel Foucault, *Power/Knowledge* (New York: Pantheon, 1980), p. 244.

9. Foucault, 1976, p. 216.

10. Foucault, 1976, p. 220.

11. B. Bernstein, "Social Class, Language, and Socialization," in Pier Paolo Giglioli, ed., *Language and Social Context* (Middlesex, Eng.: Penguin, 1972).

12. See, e.g., Roland Barthes, *Mythologies* (New York: Hill & Wang, 1972); idem, *The Pleasures of the Text* (New York: Hill & Wang, 1975); and idem, *Writing Degree Zero, and Elements of Semiology* (Boston: Beacon Press, 1968).

13. Foucault, 1976, p. 219.

14. Foucault, 1976, p. 220.

15. Foucault, 1976, p. 229.

16. Foucault, 1976, p. 230.

17. Foucault, 1976.

18. Particularly Lukács' early work, as *The Theory of The Novel* (Cambridge, Mass.: MIT Press, 1971).

19. Foucault, 1972, p. 230.

20. Foucault, 1972, p. 142–45.

The Durkheimian and Weberian Discourses 7

With Michel Foucault's work the idea of a system based on Saussurian semiotics reached its furthest development. Once ''truth'' is seen as a contingency of a discourse based on the arbitrariness of linguistic signs and political pressures, its wholly tentative character is exposed. This radical challenge to logical positivism was recognized very early in the century. In 1923, shortly after Saussure's death, C. K. Ogden and I. A. Richards published *The Meaning of Meaning*,[1] which included a blistering attack on Saussurian linguistics in its opening pages. Bronislaw Malinowski contributed a chapter to assert the anthropological authority for the position. Inspired by the work of C. S. Pierce and others, Ogden and Richards sought a positive, pragmatic approach to a science of signs in which things, rather than mentalistic concepts, are referenced by words. Since the work combined linguistic, philosophical, and psychological orientations with a strongly experimental emphasis, it remained for several decades an authoritative source for the social sciences. It was supplemented in 1946 by Charles Morris's *Signs, Language, and Behavior*.[2] Building on the work of Ogden and Richards, Morris sought to incorporate social-behaviorist insights, including those of his mentor, George Herbert Mead, whose lectures he had compiled and published as *Mind, Self, and Society*. Strongly influenced by the work of the American linguist Leonard Bloomfield, who was developing a positive form of structuralism in linguistics, Morris cited Rudolf Carnap, Hans Reichenbach, and Harold Lasswell as having provided him with additional inspiration.[3]

The tradition in semiotics represented by Ogden, Richards, and Morris has exerted considerable influence in the development of contemporary American social thought. Charles Osgood and colleagues, who devised the semantic differential and co-authored *The Measurement of Meaning*, come out of this linguistic tradition. So does Herbert Blumer and his disciples, who label themselves "symbolic interactionists." Oddly enough, these works are cited by American psychiatrist Thomas Szasz, whose *Myth of Mental Illness* assumes a position with respect to madness not unlike that championed by Foucault. R. D. Laing's early work, particularly *Interpersonal Perception*,[4] also acknowledges this tradition. In contemporary linguistics it has a spokesman in Noam Chomsky, who invokes Bloomfield and disclaims any influence by Saussure. The Ogden-Richards-Morris theory of signs formed the basis for Robert Freed Bales' *Interaction Process Analysis* (IPA) and related efforts,[5] which provided the impetus for the theory of family structure which Talcott Parsons incorporated into his general theory of action. It was while employing Bales' IPA that Harold Garfinkel arrived at his *ethnomethodology*. The work of Fred Strodtbeck, Edward Shils, Erving Goffman, and a host of other American sociologists all reflect the pragmatic, empirical, positivist treatment of language developed by the Ogden-Richards-Morris school.

From the theoretical perspective of Foucault, these authors, taken together, are engaged in a common mode of discourse, for all the surface differences that appear to separate some of them. It is a discourse at odds with that of the Saussurians. They have chosen an alternative set of paradigmatic relations within which to make their extended statements. If we at times see points of coincidence between their work and the work of the Saussurians—for example, Szasz's treatment of madness and Foucault's—this does not imply that one of these discourses may be mapped to the other in any direct way. Some chance overlapping of linguistic relations may at times apply, but these are insufficient to constitute a transformation of any kind, although such transformations between discourses do, of course, exist.

The idea of a transformation, allowing one to relate two independent systems, originated in the natural sciences and mathematics. The Lorentz transformation, for example, is a formulation of modern physics which makes it possible to move from one system of coordinates in space and time to another system of coordinates in space and time without doing injury to either system.[6] It has proven useful in the ex-

plication of relativistic phenomena. It is related to the notion of transformation employed by certain positivist structuralists, notably Noam
Chomsky, and finds application in a variety of linguistic analyses.

However, no transformation is capable of dealing with discontinui-
ties. The idea of a transformation as developed in the natural sciences
presupposes that the two systems to be related are coexisting continua,
two extended syntagms that the transformation may map, one to another. A transformation of this kind makes one system denumerable in
terms of the elements of the other. It cannot deal with morphogenetic
phenomena unless these are expressible functions of two or more otherwise continuous series. Hence, a true transformation between positivistic theories of language and Saussure's relationalism does not seem
possible.

There is, then, an inherent contradiction in the work of Lévi-Strauss
and some French structuralists that is often ignored or neglected. The
search for positive, general, nomothetic laws is at odds with the arbitrary nature of the signifier and its mutability. Nomothetic laws may
exist only *within* a discourse, that is, the relations articulated may make
other contingencies necessary and sufficient within the discourse. This
is a consequence of what we call grammar. Various sets of signs or
various discourses using signs, linguistic or otherwise, involve some
kind of grammar that functions in the form of nomothetic rules. From
this standpoint, grammar is another of the internal constraints operating on discourse. Thus, when we consider ideas there are two levels
of analysis we must take into account. The first of these is the grammar of *la langue*, the kind of grammar our teachers sought to impress
upon us, and the second is the grammar of the discourse. If I say "See
the point?" and you answer "Sure, but not always, is it?" our grammar teacher might be outraged, but we are engaged in a legitimate form
of discourse in which our meanings are mutually understood. Similarly, if I base a discourse on the omnipotence of the relations to production, or the equality of women to men, or the arbitrariness of the
division of labor, certain other predicates follow that are inevitable
consequences of my first principles. There is a grammar of meaning.
It is accordingly heretical in Marxist discourse to consider that Marx-
ists suffer from an excess of false consciousness, or within feminism
to assert that feminism is sexism and penis envy. These assertions necessarily outrage those engaged in such discourses since they belie their
first principles, the subjects of their grammatical predicates. Indeed, to

their signifiers they seem illogical, prejudiced contradictions of what to them is common sense. We become trapped in discourse and constrained to certain sets of relations by the rules of their grammars. This second level shapes discourses and history more strongly than the first.

Nomotheticism may apply within a discourse, then, but not *between* discourses. If the same set of rules applies to two or more discourses, then these discourses are truly one and the same whatever their professions. Between independent discourses some variety of transformation may be possible, however, allowing us to move between them.

Even a structuralist discourse has no direct relation to the object world. It can be positivist only in this limited, internal sense. This gives to it whatever order it seems to possess. And it is precisely this order that Foucault attacks. Foucault is saying that what social science explores is its own discourse, not the world. This is not solipsism so long as language is viewed as a collective product embodied in a particular tongue that is employed by the individuals engaged in that discourse. Just as *parole* operates by exclusion, so Foucault says discourses operate by exclusion, by purposively omitting relevant cases. Once so excluded, we are shut off from other possibilities when we attempt to engage in that discourse.

The implications of Foucault's radical critique of social science cannot be fully appreciated until we apply the method to social theory itself. In the remainder of this chapter we will play the devil's advocate and apply the principles to two quite vulnerable sociological theses and see where this leads.

For the first example we consider the violence done to our understanding of Western society by Max Weber's classic, *The Protestant Ethic and the Spirit of Capitalism*. The emergence of modern Western capitalism is held to be a consequence of the rational processes associated with the emergence of Calvinistic Protestantism in the sixteenth century. An otherworldly mysticism gave way to an innerworldly asceticism and the Puritan view of business as a vocation. Despite the objections of Tawney that in England at least capitalism had a much longer period of development, antedating the Reformation,[7] and in disregard of the weight of evidence provided by other historians than those Weber chose as his sources, the very magnitude of Weber's undertaking imparted an authoritative air that few social scientists were willing or able to challenge. College professors involved in sociological discourses have by now indoctrinated legions of college students into the belief that something called "the Protestant work ethic" is responsible for the rampant abuses of modern capitalism. Indeed, this notion is now part of popular culture, along with other Weberian notions such as "life-style" and "charisma."

Capitalism, for Weber, was a kind of *geist* evolving in the world as a consequence of a distinctively Western rationality. When a religious belief came about embodying this rationality, it *caused* the emergence of modern Western capitalism. Weber is very specific about the direction of this causal linkage. In what now appears as the "Author's Introduction" in the Talcott Parsons translation of the *Protestant Ethic*[8]—which may very well be the last thing Weber ever wrote[9] and in which he attempts to understand the pattern of his life's work—Weber tells us that these essays seek to grasp "the influence of certain religious ideas on the development of an economic spirit, or the ethos of an economic system. In this case we are dealing with the connection of the spirit of modern economic life with the rational ethics of ascetic protestantism. Thus we treat here only one side of the causal chain."[10] Here it is the religious ideas that causally affect developments in the economic spirit; more than simple correlation is involved, for both the direction of influence and its status within a causal chain are asserted. Because he is engaged here in causal analysis of the natural science variety,[11] Weber finds it necessary to remind us that the treatment afforded in the *Protestant Ethic* is only "one side of the causal chain." The other side of the causal chain is accordingly the absence of these specific religious ideas precluding the development of this form of capitalism. He treats this side in his other works on the sociology of religion.

If we take up his proposition, we see that there are two variables and therefore four logical possibilities. Let PE = Protestant ethic and SC = spirit of capitalism, and the absence be indicated by a bar. Then,

1. $\text{PE} \rightarrow \text{SC}$
2. $\overline{\text{PE}} \rightarrow \overline{\text{SC}}$
3. $\overline{\text{PE}} \rightarrow \text{SC}$
4. $\text{PE} \rightarrow \overline{\text{SC}}$

Weber must show that 1 and 2 are true but 3 and 4 are not. That is, where he finds the Protestant ethic he finds also the spirit of capitalism, and where he does not find the Protestant ethic he does not find

Figure 7.1
Truth Table of the *Protestant Ethic* Thesis

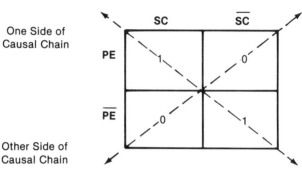

the spirit of capitalism. However, this is only one side of the chain, corresponding to 1 and 2. The other side corresponds to hypotheses 3 and 4, that is, where he may find the spirit of capitalism but the Protestant ethic is absent, or the Protestant ethic with the spirit of capitalism absent. In binary logic, this leads to the truth table of Figure 7.1. The cells in which we show 1's should have empirical existence; that is, one should be able to find societies of this kind; but one should not be able to find empirical examples of the kinds shown by cells with a zero.

This is what Weber claimed to be attempting to demonstrate. From a structuralist standpoint we see that Weber is confined within a particular rationalistic discourse. In such a discourse, events cannot occur by chance, as in Foucault's *discontinuity*, but must be causally linked to other phenomena, phenomena of the same kind, as Fauconnet would say. Weber accordingly struggles with the impossibility of demonstrating such a concrete causal connection with abstract entities such as a "spirit" and an "ethos." We can appreciate this struggle by his attempt, in the "Author's Introduction," to move them down to a lower level of abstraction than they are in the text itself.

Weber begins by defining *capitalism* as the rational pursuit of profit in peaceful exchange[12] where the calculation is in terms of money value,[13] but he concludes that this has always existed in civilized countries of the past, including China and India.[14] He then defines a subset of capitalism which he terms "Western capitalism,"[15] involving rational organization and personal property, typical of the medieval period in Europe.[16] Within this subset he then defines a subset which he terms "modern Western capitalism," involving the rational organization of free labor.[17] This set, subset, and sub-subset are shown in the Venn diagram of Figure 7.2. Weber informs us that this last characteristic is necessary because modern Western capitalism is only possible on the basis of accurate labor cost calculations. The dependent variable of the four hypotheses listed above is to be searched for employing all the elements of the complete set shown in Figure 7.2, that is, the pursuit of profit in peaceful exchange where the calculations are in terms of money, where such activity involves rational organization attuned to a regular market and the rational organization of formally free labor. Since the subset A' is, on Weber's own terms, known to have been present in medieval Europe and therefore to have pre-dated the emergence of Protestantism, one would suppose that all that needs be demonstrated is that the emergence of Protestantism was a consequence of the rational organization of free labor (see Figure 7.2), making the sub-subset A", modern Western capitalism, possible. But Weber never makes this connection, and the enterprise flounders as he seeks the other half of the causal chain of Figure 7.1. He embarks on an infinite regression into the sources of rationality in Western and non-Western societies.

A reduction of the argument to the truth table of Figure 7.1 leads to other complications. The table can show only correlation, not causality. In addition, there is no way, by employing such a methodology, that the *direction* of causality can be shown once correlation is established unless temporal sequencing leads us to assume a direction. The absence of correlation may show the absence of causality, as in the zeros of the truth table, but the reverse need not be true unless some positive epistemic correlation can be assumed and a temporal priority established between variables.[18]

Had Weber followed the rationalist imperatives of his own discourse, he would have sought to show a causal connection with the distinguishing characteristic of the sub-subset A" of the Venn diagram of Figure 7.2, it being established that A' and A were already present in medieval Europe. This would have moved him away from such highly abstract concepts as a "spirit" and an "ethos" to the less abstract "free labor" and "modern Western capitalism." The truth table for this is shown in Figure 7.3. We see that either free labor led to modern Western capitalism or modern Western capitalism led to free labor. These are phenomena of the same kind which may be shown to have causal

Figure 7.2

Max Weber's Concepts of Capitalism Shown as a
Set and a Venn Diagram

(A   (A'   (A")))

(b)

A = The pursuit of profit in peaceful exchange where the calculations are in terms
of money, i.e., *capitalism*

A' = Such activity as (A) involving rational organization attuned to a regular market,
i.e., *Western capitalism*

A" = Such activity as (A') involving the rational organization of formally free labor,
i.e., *modern Western capitalism*

Figure 7.3

Improved Truth Table of the Thesis

	MWC	$\overline{\text{MWC}}$
FL	1	0
FL	0	1

FL   = Free labor
MWC = Modern Western capitalism

connection, while the abstract "ethos" and "spirit" clearly cannot. Again, neither causality nor its direction can be shown by mere correlation. But since we know that free labor existed in Europe prior to Luther and Calvin, we might hypothesize that FL → MWC could have occurred, and by examination fail to reject the hypothesis. Whether or not religious ideas were changing in terms of asceticism and mysticism (and they had been for at least a thousand years, as the history of Christian heresies shows) has nothing whatever to do with the hypothesis. It would seem more reasonable, from the standpoint of a rationalistic ordered discourse, to assume that once free labor emerged, capitalism was quick to seize upon it and include its costs in the rational calculative activity characteristic of it in A'. The Protestant spirit, once it emerged, can be expected to have employed the exploitive capitalistic ethic that had always existed.

What Weber excludes in his paradigmatic selections that comprise the syntagms of his discourse is the Protestant spirit and the ethics of capitalism. Proceeding as he was on an anti-Marxist thesis, he accordingly minimized those exploitive ethics of capitalism that had outraged Marx. Perhaps he hesitated to treat the abuses of capitalism because he was claiming a Protestant origin for its contemporary form and in Protestant Germany.

If we are wedded to this variety of historicism, then Foucault's insight respecting *reversal* clarifies the matter for us at once. A chance historical occurrence—the Black Death—decimated the population of Europe and the British Isles and led to fragmentation of the manorial economy. Free labor came about, as in England, as increasing numbers of serfs were freed from feudal obligations by their lords and were forced to sell their labor in order to survive.[19] In England, as on the Continent, there were sufficient entrepreneurs to seize upon the monetary consequences. This does not require the monumental discourse of a Max Weber.

Recently Jere Cohen has presented convincing data from a quite different quarter.[20] He shows that all the elements of the set, subset and sub-subset of Figure 7.2 were already present in Roman Catholic Italy long before the Reformation and that any causal connection between what Weber defines as the emergence of ''modern Western capitalism'' and the emergence of Protestantism is a spurious relationship and must be dismissed. Empirical evidence for hypothesis 3, $\overline{PE} \rightarrow SC$ exists.

The preceding discussion will annoy the Weberians, who will rightly claim that we have ignored what Weber says elsewhere. This objection cannot hold, however, since what we have examined are Weber's last words on what he intended to say; whether he contradicts himself elsewhere is not important. Here we have invoked the *sovereignty of the signifier*. His work has become a variety of *commentary* for sociologists, an orthodoxy where commentators argue about his precise meaning.[21] It is typical of the attempt to ''burrow to the core of meaning'' in Foucault's terms, a failure to employ a judicious *exteriority* of the kind here employed. In seeing the violence Weber did to the ''things examined,'' we imposed our own violence upon his discourse and ''made more sense'' of the available data. This is what Foucault refers to as *specificity*. In rejecting the causal connection between Protestantism and capitalism, we followed Foucault's assertion that ''it is clearly no longer possible to establish . . . causal links [and] . . . we must accept the introduction of chance as a category'' in his definition of *discontinuity*. His principle of *reversal* encouraged us to consider how free labor led to the phenomenon to be explained, rather than some abstract ethic or spirit grounded in religion. Of course, Weber supplies the discontinuity himself by making the distinguishing feature of modern Western capitalism *free labor* and then failing to treat it as the key element determining the dependent variable.

Weberian sociology is a rich discourse that immerses itself in the beauties of language without understanding the nature of language as Saussure reveals it for us. For this reason it is particularly vulnerable to the kind of attack structuralism can offer. Since it deals with dia-chronic phenomena at the level of the emergence of ideas, the method-ology of Foucault seems particularly appropriate to its analysis.

This places sociologists intent on exploring the implications of structuralism for authoritative social theory in a position not unlike that of Jack the Giant-killer. A Weberian canon exists within contemporary social thought, and to some it appears heretical to challenge it on the basis of an idea of a system predicated on semiological signs, partic-ularly since this has emerged in French social thought, generally rec-ognized as being quite a distinct mode of discourse from the German. Having done violence to Weber, therefore, it appears equally appro-priate now to do violence to Durkheim. Fortunately this is a much eas-ier task, for the discourse is not as extended and the synchronic treat-ment he furnished is closer to the Saussurian treatment than is the discourse of the Weberians.

To appreciate the simplicity of a structuralist attack upon the Dur-kheimian schema, we can employ a highly trivial form of Saussurian structuralism. This version owes its origins to Phillip Pettit, a follower of Chomsky who generally misreads the *Course* and vigorously attacks Lévi-Strauss and other ''antiphenomenalists,'' such as Foucault.[22] For example, Pettit misreads Saussure's description of the linguistic sign, making it only the complete word.[23] Accordingly, for Pettit only com-plete sentences constitute syntagms.[24] Once this approach is taken, Pettit insists that signs other than words cannot be treated as elements of a system of signs unless they can be read as a sentence! Taken together, he says, Lévi-Strauss's kinship terms do not constitute such a sentence and therefore cannot be treated as a system of signs.[25] Accordingly, Pettit reduces the paradigmatic relation to such word substitutions in complete sentences that allow the sentence to continue to make some kind of sense.

While this is a trivial view of Saussurian semiotics, this reduction-istic form can be quite useful for nonlinguistic signs. A cuisine allows for such a system of signs constituting a sentence, since particular dishes must be eaten in a certain order, and there is a paradigmatic choice among menu dishes for each course.[26] For example, a dinner may have the form

shrimp cocktail → salad → steak & potatoes →apple pie → coffee

This is a complete statement with a beginning and an end. Each of the courses serves the same function as a word in a sentence. The dinner reads from left to right. It begins with the shrimp cocktail as an appetizer, intended to whet one's appetite for the coming elements of the syntagmatic chain. The salad provides the fresh greens to take one gently into the dinner's real substance. The steak and potatoes serve this function of substantiality; it is here one finds the stress in the meaning of the meal. The apple pie, a dessert, is to provide sweetness as a last touch of food, a function opposite that of the salad. The coffee provides a light re-stimulation after the heaviness of the meal.

We have no difficulty recognizing this as an American dinner. The paradigmatic relations of each element is also apparent. The choice of shrimp cocktail eliminates other possible appetizers, such as relishes or soups (although in an extended syntagm these might be included as elements of the sequence, in which case other paradigmatic relations result). And various kinds of salad are excluded by the choice of salad one makes: a Caesar salad, chef's salad, lettuce and tomato, cucumber, and so on. The entree could be chicken and dumplings, or pork chops and applesauce, or something else of substance, even fish. Dessert could be ice cream, chocolate layer cake, or a pastry of some kind. A simple, two-dimensional matrix of possibilities results, as in Figure 7.4. This should be compared with Figure 4.1 in Chapter 4.

Such a dinner sentence varies among different cultural groups, a function of the cuisine (the equivalent of *la langue*) in both syntagmatic sequence and the specific dishes available for a particular course. In French or Italian dinners, for example, the salad is likely to come *after* the entree and not *before* it, as the adjective comes after the noun and not before it in these languages. The culinary art of the various cultures provides menus of various entrees, appetizers, desserts, and beverages for paradigmatic variations.

A tour through a museum may also be analyzed in such a fashion. As one passes through the various rooms, one constructs a sentence; as one pauses to include one statue, one excludes other statues, just as the choice of fish excludes steak or chicken. Various syntagmatic sentences may be constructed within one museum, depending on the rooms selected, the sequence in which it is selected, and the things excluded by the selection. Barry Schwartz has analyzed statuary in the United States Capitol building in this fashion, although at this writing the analysis remains unpublished.

Figure 7.4

Syntagmatic and Paradigmatic Dimensions of a Dinner

Syntagmatic dimension →

	1. Appetizer	2. Greens	3. Entree	4. Dessert	5. Beverage
Syntagm:	—Shrimp cocktail—	—Salad—	—Steak & potatoes—	—Apple pie—	—Coffee— → Paradigmatic dimension
	Soup	Endive	Chicken & dumplings	Torte	Tea
	Relishes	Olives & celery	Stuffed Dover sole	Pudding	Milk
	Oysters	Pâté de fois gras	Duck	Parfait	Espresso
	Clams	Cole slaw	Lobster	Spumoni	Anisette

Time →

One's clothing, head to foot, may have such an order to it also, according to Pettit. The particular articles selected exclude other possibilities. If one is required to "dress" for work, one first selects the suit, then the tie and socks to go with it, then the shoes, and so on.

One does not do violence to Saussurian semiotics with this simplistic model, so long as one does not insist that this is all Saussure intends. Signs are more subtle than these gross categories indicate. In cuisine this helps make the difference between broiled fish, boiled fish, and fried fish. And what sort of dressing does one wish on one's salad? French? Italian? Cheese? Thousand Island? Russian? In ties it makes the difference between a "cheap tie" and a "good tie," a silk tie, wool tie, cotton tie, foulard, bow, string, straight, striped, checked, dotted, plaid, and an infinite range of colors. One may gloss over these distinctions and treat the elements wholly abstractly (a tie? what one uses to close a plastic garbage bag? sack? container?), disregarding possibly distinctive qualities of meaning linked to the signifier. This makes of semiology a simple variety of grammar: a noun is not an adjective, nor is it a verb. But while Saussure does not dismiss grammar, he treats it summarily.[27] He is interested in more than the substitution of one word for another, one dish for another, although allowing for it.

In this matter of the nonlinguistic sentence, we confront a problem of another kind. Although the "sentence structure" of the dinner example clearly comprises a syntagmatic series that is unidirectional in time, one starting at appetizer and ending with coffee, in the case of attire or clothing it does not. This is significant because attire is one category of signs with which Pettit deals. I can read the signs of attire of a man (or a woman) from head to toe or toe to head. However, sometimes in reading the signs of clothing of a woman, for example, I start somewhere in-between. The total *gestalt*, after all, is what clothing is all about, not lineal ordering. When we read the signs of clothing, we are closer to what Lévi-Strauss does with kinship terms than to what Pettit wants us to do. We are looking for relationships *among* the various signs, sometimes considering the shoes with the hat, the shoes with the skirt, the scarf with the blouse or with the color of the hair or with both. These operations do not comprise sentences.

If one were to go fishing, for example, and catch a large fish, one might broil the entire fish and eat it with only some rolls and coffee; if one were camping and lacked refrigeration, this might be the only possibility. In this case, the fish is not a snack, but one's *dinner*. Any system of signs of cuisine must make allowances for just such likelihoods. It does so if it closely follows Saussure, for the dinner "sentence" begins when one starts to ingest food and ceases when one ceases to ingest food. The ordering is provided by the intentionality of the actor-eater, not by the external courses as "things in themselves." *Dinner* is first and foremost a pair of linguistic signs in English, *din* and *ner*. If one says, "Last night my wife and I shared a very large fish for *dinner* at camp," one is imposing his intentionality upon the set of possible signifiers in English in order to communicate some meaning. This meaning is not a property of the words themselves, but of a common understanding among members of a speech community; the meaning belongs to the system, to *langue*, not to *parole*. If you are a member of this speech community, you should have minimal difficulty understanding the intention behind the sounds. If you have doubts, you might make the nonsentence reply "A fish?" or "Only a fish?" and the speaker might reply with the nonsentence nod of his head. You two understand one another. That, Saussure reminds us, is what language is all about; it is not simply about grammatical sentences nor about external things.

We can carry this one step further and illustrate a quite different point. One can say "A car rides on the road." But if one substitutes *boat* for *car* the sentence is not acceptable. To make it acceptable one must also substitute *water* for *road*. A car rides on the road, a boat rides on the water, a train rides on the rails, an airplane rides on air, and so on. We can write this sentence (Figure 7.5) in the same form as our

Figure 7.5

Syntagmatic and Paradigmatic Dimensions in a Simple Sentence

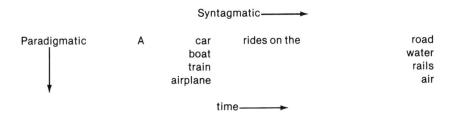

other examples. Saussure says we memorize useful groups like this: A
(   ) *rides on the* (   ). It is certainly the easiest way of learning travelers' languages. We memorize "Où on s'il trouvé (   )?"
in French, the useful "Dovè (   )?" in Italian, or "*Where is*
(   )? in English, and fill in the blanks as the need arises, with the
word for washroom, or the street name, and so forth.

Note that when the first blank of A (   ) *rides on the* (   )
is specified, our choice for the second blank is either given directly or
highly limited. If one chooses *boat* for the first blank, *water* must be
chosen for the second blank; if one chooses either *lake, ocean, river,*
or *bay* for the second blank, he is less correct, for what a boat rides
on that is common to all these is *water*, and nothing else. This is dictated by the use of the indefinite article in English; had the definite
article *the* been employed, one of the other alternatives may have made
an acceptable sentence.

This is an example of a simple kind of transformation. One is relat-
ing different kinds of craft by their appropriate media. Once the craft
is designated, the medium is at once given. A car is to a road what a
boat is to the water, Lévi-Strauss would say.

If we take a syntagmatic string of the type shown in figure 7.5, and
change its subject, its predicate changes. This seems to hold for any
semiological system. Once the color of the suit is selected, only certain shirts and ties go with it. The dinner sentence has the entree as its
subject, all else being structured about it. A shrimp cocktail would not
be followed by an anchovy salad, a tuna fish sandwich, and a fish as-
pic unless one does not know cuisine. If one can be satisfied with a
tuna fish sandwich as one's entree, a light tossed salad and perhaps
some tea and biscuits would "go with it." There are paradigmatic
possibilities at each step, but not all are as likely or acceptable. Some
are even positively demanded either by the grammar of the semiological system or that of the discourse. It is at this point that we come to
Durkheim.

In *The Elementary Forms of the Religious Life*, Durkheim goes to
great pains to show that when aboriginal people find themselves conscious of something greater than themselves, which they refer to as
God, what they are really conscious of is the power and presence of
their collectivity.[28] The order they perceive in the world is their communal, social order, which is external to them but exerts an influence
on them. This is a necessary extension of the thesis proposed by Dur-

kheim and Mauss in *Primitive Classification*; the classification of things reflects the classification of men.

What Durkheim has done here is propose a transformation of the same kind as when one substitutes *boat* for *car*. If we take the orthodox Christian statement "God is that within which we live and move and have our being," for example, and replace *God* with *Society*, the sentence makes sense even without changing the signs in the predicate, although what these signs now mean is something quite different. From Durkheim's theoretical standpoint, "Society is that within which we live and move and have our being." In the variety of Christian theology to which Durkheim was everywhere exposed, a metaphysical principle obtains objectification in the real world (see Figure 7.6). Estrangement from this objectification can be at the individual and/or the collective level, that is, *sin* and/or *hell*. One proceeds in this system of signs by sets of binary oppositions that define the limits of each function. The binary pair *sin/hell* stands in opposition to the binary pair *grace/heaven*. In Lévi-Strauss's terms we would say: *Sin is to hell as grace is to heaven*. Some of these relations are spelled out in Table 7.1. There is the Old Testament based on blood relations, and the New Testament based on a direct relation to God, and so on.

Once *God = Society* is asserted as a transformation between orthodox Christian theology and the new sociology, the Durkheimian schema falls into place automatically and is fully developed. The Old Testament or convenant based on blood relations becomes *mechanical solidarity*, the New Testament or covenant based on a functional relationship to God becomes *organic solidarity*. *Deviance* is to *moral integration* what *sin* is to *grace*. Hence, if God = Society, then *sin = deviance*, *grace = moral integration* in this new secular theology. Using the transformation God = Society, a one-to-one mapping is possible between orthodox Christian signifiers and the Durkheimian signifiers.[29] The Durkheimian mode of discourse attempts to recapture medieval Christian discourse. Sociologists become high priests of a new secular religion, fulfilling the Saint-Simonean dream. Fauconnet, by making the actor responsible, makes him capable of committing sin.

We can make too much of this. But Durkheim, after all, walked where Abelard had walked, taught where Thomas Aquinas and his mentor Albert Magnus had taught, at the university in Paris. When Durkheim renounced his inherited Judaism, he was already in process of developing this new Christian sociology of moral integration, com-

Figure 7.6

The Deeper Structure of the Durkheimian Transformation

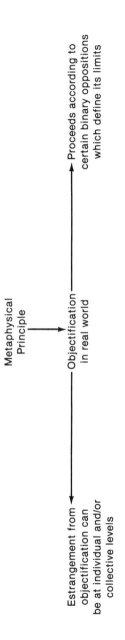

Metaphysical Principle

Objectification in real world

Estrangement from objectification can be at individual and/or collective levels

Proceeds according to certain binary oppositions which define its limits

The deeper structure of the Durkheimian transformation equating God and Society. In both Durkheimian sociology and Medieval Christian theology, "the word is made flesh," i.e., some metaphysical principle (society, God), becomes the basis of objectification. At both the individual and collective levels, estrangement from this objectification is possible, if not demanded by the objectification itself. Thus it creates the conditions for its own binary oppositions. Its central organization as a discourse is specified by the transformed binary pairs, e.g., Old vs. New Covenant, mechanical vs. organic solidarity, and so on. See text.

Table 7.1

The Christian Orthodoxy of Durkheim's Sociology

DURKHEIM'S SOCIOLOGY		CHRISTIAN ORTHODOXY
Transformation:	Society =	God
Central principle:	Of its own kind, more than the sum of its parts	One creator of all things; plural but singular
Organization:	Division of labor (mediating structure between individuals and society)	Church universal (mediating structure between individuals and God)
Presence in individuals:	Collective conscience (society within us)	Holy Spirit (God within us)
Basis of moral community:	Social integration (membership in and identification with mediating structure)	Church membership (membership in and identification with mediating structure)
Oppositions (govern relations within system):	Mechanical solidarity (old normative order of blood relations, kinship)	Old Covenant or Testament (old normative order of blood relations, kinship)
	vs.	vs.
	Organic solidarity (new normative order with direct functional relationship to society)	New Covenant or Testament (new normative order with direct functional relationship to God)
Negation of governing relations		
1. Individual level:	Deviance (vs. moral integration)	Sin (vs. grace)
2. Collective level:	Anomie (estrangement from society) vs. integration within society	Hell (estrangement from God) vs. Heaven, nearness to God.
3. Others, e.g.:	Sacred vs. profane Moral vs. physical	"Render unto Caesar what is Caesar's unto God what is God's."
Misc.	"a community of saints is impossible"	"Let him among you who is without sin cast the first stone."

117

munion with society. Lévi-Strauss invites us to consider the unconscious as a contributing explanation for the associations among signs, and perhaps in this instance it is peculiarly rewarding.

The linguistic signs of Durkheim's sociology, the theoretical concepts linking and interrelating the Durkheimian schema, are neither analogies nor metaphors. Each signifier performs the identical function as the signifier it replaces in the earlier discourse and makes the new discourse possible.

That Durkheimian discourse may be mapped on a one-to-one basis with medieval Christian discourse by means of a simple transformation should not surprise us. Norman Cohen has suggested relations between its predecessor, Comtean discourse, and that of the medievalists.[30] He finds that Comte's three stages of theology, metaphysics, and science remarkably reiterate the three stages in the eschatology of Joachim of Fiore, the Franciscan mystic: Law, Revelation, and Spirit. Aquinas at Paris had opposed Fiore's eschatology, which Cohen calls "the prophetic system which was to be the most influential one known in Europe until the appearance of Marxism."[31] Thus Durkheim had precedents for his transformation.

That certain iterative structured patterns exist in speculative discourses is, of course, well known. They give every indication of being a pattern of articulation imposed upon us by our categorization. The three-stage structure is historically frequent, particularly in social science. D. C. Phillips, in his discussion of holism, cites John Dewey's three stages of *self-action*, *interaction*, and *transaction*;[32] Robert Park had his *association*, *accommodation*, and *assimilation*. These are seen as evolutionary stages of development similar to those of Comte and Fiore. Zimmermann finds three similar evolutionary stages in Lukács's *Theory of the Novel* (1920) and in Victor Hugo's *Preface de Cromwell* (1827).[33] And of course there is always the Hegelian evolutionary trio of thesis, antithesis, and synthesis.

In analyzing Durkheim's schema in this way, we have performed a variety of structural analysis not unlike that performed by Lévi-Strauss in his analysis of kinship terms. We have also employed Foucault's two principles of *exteriority* and *reversal*. From this perspective, what Durkheim presents to us is a way of speaking about the elementary forms of the socio-semiological life. These elementary forms are readily isolated because of the synchronic character of this sociology.

Such an analysis will offend Durkheimians, as the discussion of

Weber's *Protestant Ethic* will offend Weberians, but for quite different reasons. The principal source of irritation will be the conclusion that what is perceived as contemporary structuralism may be derived from the work of Durkheim and his followers virtually independent of the work of Saussure. Here we turn the system back on itself in the manner of the anti-Freudians who employ Freudian explanations to discredit the explanations of Freudians. But this property lies dormant in all discourses; when it lies close to the surface we do not hesitate to label such a discourse "ideology." The fact that structuralist methods such as these enable us to penetrate social-scientific discourses, including the history of ideas and sociological theories, points to the method's usefulness.

A methodology is useful to the extent that it reveals new plausibilities, ones we may tentatively accept and operate with to further our understanding.[34] According to Popper in his debate with Adorno, this is not only what positivism is all about, it is also what science is all about.[35]

This chapter has applied some "structuralist" methods to theoretical literatures of two different kinds. Both are authoritative bodies, embodying *commentary*, the *disciplines*, and both *internal* and *external* constraints that limit one's participation within them. In doing violence to them we have done no more than what any analytical procedure does to that which it treats: it destroys its apparent unity and wholeness for the sake of understanding its internal structure. It does this to extract meanings that are not apparent to casual observation. Whether what it extracts is "true" in any sense other than as a set of relations within the discourse remains uncertain, for here too one is employing a discourse, with all its limitations, internal and external constraints.

Notes

1. C. K. Ogden and I. A. Richards, *The Meaning of Meaning* (New York: Harcourt Brace, 1923).

2. Charles Morris, *Signs, Language, and Behavior* (New York: Braziller, 1946).

3. Morris's acknowledgments include most of the major behaviorists of his day.

4. R. D. Laing, H. Phillipson, and A. R. Lee, *Interpersonal Perception* (New York: Harper & Row, 1966).

5. See Chapter 2, note 28, for the IPA literature.

6. Galileo concluded that the motion of a projectile launched at any angle could be derived from its motion when launched straight up. This became the basis of the "Galileo transformation." It does not hold at speeds near the speed of light, however. When two frames of reference are moving with respect to each other at such velocities, the Lorentz transformation becomes necessary. For a discussion, see Robert Katz, *An Introduction to the Special Theory of Relativity* (New York: Van Nostrand, 1964).

7. Some of Tawney's objections are contained in the foreword of the Parsons' translation, cited below.

8. Max Weber, *The Protestant Ethic and the Spirit of Capitalism*, trans. Talcott Parsons (New York: Scribner's, 1958).

9. In 1920, the year of Weber's death. For a discussion of the significance of this, see Benjamin Nelson, "Max Weber's 'Author's Introduction' (1920): A Master Clue to His Main Aims," *Sociological Inquiry* 44(1), 1974; see also Benjamin Nelson, "Weber's Protestant Ethic: Its Origins, Wanderings, and Foreseeable Futures," in Charles Y. Glock and Phillip E. Hammond, eds., *Beyond the Classics?* (New York: Harper & Row, 1973).

10. Weber, 1958, p. 27.

11. See Fauconnet's distinction with respect to causality in Chapter 5.

12. Weber, 1958, p. 17.

13. Weber, 1958, p. 19.

14. Weber, 1958, p. 19.

15. Weber, 1958, p. 21.

16. Weber, 1958, p. 22.

17. Weber, 1958, p. 22.

18. Hubert W. Blalock, Jr., *Causal Inference in Nonexperimental Research* (Chapel Hill: University of North Carolina Press, 1969).

19. See, e.g., G. M. Trevelyan, *England in the Age of Wycliff* (London: Longmans, 1925); Helen Cam, *England Before Elizabeth* (London: Hutchinson, 1950).

20. Jere Cohen, "Rational Capitalism in Renaissance Italy," *American Journal of Sociology* 84(6), 1980.

21. See, e.g., I. Wallimann, H. Rosenbaum, N. Tatsis, and G. V. Zito, "Misreading Weber: The Concept of Macht," *Sociology: Journal of the British Sociological Association* 14(2), 1980.

22. Philip Pettit, *The Concept of Structuralism* (Berkeley: University of California Press, 1977).

23. This is odd, for Saussure repeatedly (as in his example of *de-faire* and *quadra-plex*) employs linguistic units such as *de* and *quadra* as signs.

24. This contradicts Saussure (1966), who tells us that "if in Latin *quad-raplex* is a syntagm, this is because it too is supported by a double associative series" (p. 129), that is, a series of paradigmatic associations in *quadra-* and

another series in *-plex.* The union of two or more linguistic units constitutes a syntagm: "The syntagm is always composed of two or more consecutive units (e.g., *re-lire, contre tous, la vie humain,* etc.)" (p. 123). But Pettit, 1977, p. 42, sees only sentences as syntagms.

25. Pettit, 1977, p. 70, "I shall not discuss Lévi-Strauss's analysis of kinship. It is not a semiological analysis because there is nothing in kinship to correspond properly to the sentence in language" (*sic*).

26. Pettit, 1977, p. 36, suggests the menu as a sentence, and I here elaborate on that suggestion.

27. Saussure, 1966, p. 134–39.

28. Émile Durkheim, *The Elementary Forms of the Religious Life* (New York: Free Press, 1915).

29. This has been touched on elsewhere: See George V. Zito, "Giovanni's Ladder: Early Franciscan and Social Scientific Thought," Paper delivered at the annual meeting of the Eastern Sociological Society, New York, March 1979.

30. Norman Cohen, *The Pursuit of the Millennium* (New York: Oxford University Press, 1970).

31. Norman Cohen, 1970, p. 109.

32. D. C. Phillips, *Holistic Thought in Social Science* (Stanford, Calif.: Stanford University Press, 1976), p. 51.

33. Jacquelyne Zimmermann, "Similarities Between Hugo and Lukács," unpublished paper, Cornell University, Ithaca, N.Y., October 1979.

34. George V. Zito, *Methodology and Meanings* (New York: Praeger, 1975); see also, "Toward a Sociology of Heresy," *Sociological Analysis* 44 (2), 1983.

35. Theodor Adorno, ed., *The Positivist Dispute in German Sociology* (New York: Harper & Row, 1976).

The Third System and Social Science   8

The preceding chapters have examined the idea of a system of action from several different perspectives. At this point it is appropriate to summarize them in the order considered and speculate on the contributions structuralism can make to the social sciences.

Type I: The Cause/Effect Recursive System

This type of elementary system is typified by the familiar mousetrap; however, it may attain highly sophisticated embodiments. One or more elements A, B, C, ... N, each performing some function in the operation of the system as a whole, are in linear sequence. See Figure 8.1. The input is at A and the output is at n. Since only a single input and output are provided, the mousetrap system may be represented by a single black box which includes the elements within it. See Figure 8.2. A system such as MT moves from one quiescent state s_1 to another quiescent state s_2 and must be reset to function again. Its operation takes a finite time t_0. Its output action is a step function, the movement from s_1 to s_2. See Figure 8.3. The output action can also be symbolized in binary logic notation as a movement from 0 to 1, where $s_1 = 0$ and $s_2 = 1$. Series of the black boxes of Figure 8.2 may be arranged redundantly, but the input to the first one remains the input to the system as a whole, and the output of the last one the output of the system as a whole, so the system again reduces to the single black box of Figure 8.2, producing the output shown in Figure 8.3.

Figure 8.1

Cause/Effect Recursive System

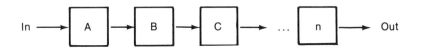

Figure 8.2

Black Box Representation of the
System of Figure 8.1

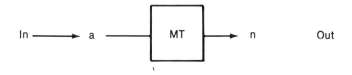

Figure 8.3

Output of the System of Figure 8.1

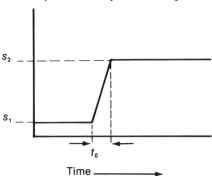

This is a fully causal action system. Once the input is activated at a (or X), then Y (or s_2) automatically follows.

Such systems are found as biological tropisms, in simulus-response theories of behaviorism, in simple theories of exchange, and in the hypothetico-deductive model. Figure 8.2 is also a binary logic element and is employed in electronic computer circuitry. The theory of such logic circuits was developed as switching logic by Shannon and employs Boolean algebra in its analysis.[1] It was subsequently incorporated into information theory.

Type II: The Cybernetic System

This type of system is typified by the familiar toy kite. It is an adaptive system, adjusting itself to its environment by modifying its performance to accommodate environmental changes. Its functional elements are in a nonrecursive sequence. This is shown in Figure 8.4. Although the input is shown at A in the figure and the output at n, inputs and outputs may be obtained at other junctions of the elements, depending on the function the system is called on to perform. In Figure 8.4 the element D provides the feedback, which is ususally in opposition to the initiating action. Other feedback paths may also exist around elements.

The system of Figure 8.4 may also be represented as a single black box with the input and output of the previous figure: see Figure 8.5.Such a system seeks to stabilize itself about some quiescent operating point s_1, if it is a stable system. This is shown by its output action. See Fig-

Figure 8.4

Cybernetic System

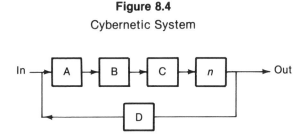

Figure 8.5

Black Box Representation of the System
of Figure 8.4

In a —·—| KT |——▶ n Out

ure 8.6. If it is unstable, it follows one of the patterns shown in Figure
2.3 of Chapter 2. Its operation takes a finite time, but the period varies
as a function of the system's displacement from s_1, as in t_0, t_1 and t_2.
Observation performed at any point in the circuit of Figure 8.4 yields
a metric that is a consequence of both the initiating cause at a and the
amount of the effect fed back from the output by D. This is only a
partially causal system, since effects modify causes and may not be
separated from them for observation and measurement. Such systems
are found in neuromuscular physiology, in fully interactive models of
small-group phenomena, in guidance and control systems of aircraft
and space vehicles, in speed governors and other industrial applications, and in the modified version of the Parsonian social system.

Figure 8.6

Output of the System of Figure 8.4

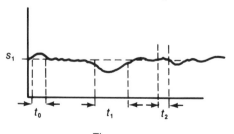

Time

Type III: The Semiotic or Semiological System

This type of system is typified by language but is applicable to a variety of sign systems. In this system a set of elements A, B, C, . . . , *n* is made available, as in Figure 8.7. Most if not all elements are related in some way with other elements of the system, although this is subject to change. Only one "plane" of elements is shown in Figure 8.7, but the matrix must be conceived as being *n*-dimensional. In operation the intentionality of the user selects a particular series of elements, such as the syntagms A, B, C, and so on, in a particular order. If this is a language system, the user articulates the sounds associated with this sequence of elements as he selects them. The system may be represented by a single black box which includes an input and an output, as in Figure 8.8. Here the input is the intentionality of the user; the output is his articulation. The output action is therefore a sequence of meaningless sounds (if this is a language system), as shown in Figure 8.9. These sounds vary in pitch, in durations (as in t_0, t_1, t_2), and in their relative position in time with respect to each other (thus the

Figure 8.7

Semiotic or Semiological System

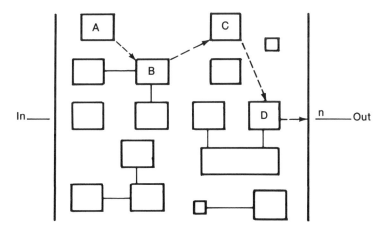

Figure 8.8
Black Box Representation of the System of Figure 8.7

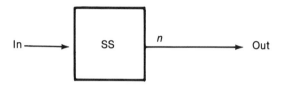

sound *a* takes longer to articulate than sound *b*, occurs earlier than it does, and is separated from sound *d* by a relatively long period, t_5).

A person with a similar (although never identical) matrix as that shown in Figure 8.7 understands these sounds of Figure 8.9 in terms of meanings. The matrix is not a product of the user but of the cultural system that developed it, and it is acquired by the user through socialization and education. The linkage between the sound image and the mental (meaning) image is arbitrary and has no relation to anything external to the system.

Since internal sets of relations and connections exist between certain elements of the system, as shown in the dark line connections of Figure 8.7 (associative or paradigmatic relations), it is these sets of internal relations, represented by the differences among them, which must be grasped by the hearer to be translatable into meanings. The ordering of these meanings, which itself conveys additional meaning (syntagmatic relations), is a function of the various time relations, t_0, t_1, t_2, t_3 as well as of t_4, t_5, and so on.

Such systems are found not only as languages, spoken and written, but also in other sets of signs, such as those of cuisine or of dress, and in theoretical formulations of discourse, such as sociological theory, economic theory, psychological theory, and so on, as well as in ideological rhetorics, systems of philosophical thought, interpretive histories, museum collections, department store displays, and wherever systems of interrelated signs are made available.

The system of Figure 8.8 is not a causal system of the Type I or Type II systems. If we are satisfied with referencing the Type II sys-

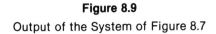

Figure 8.9

Output of the System of Figure 8.7

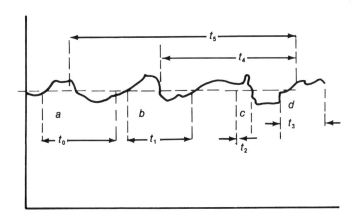

Time ⟶

tems as only partially causal because of our inability to separate by measurement and observation its compounded cause and effect metric, then we must consider the Type III system as a noncausal system. It is causal only to the extent that its operation is a function of the intentionality of the user who orders its elements syntagmatically. He is accordingly the cause of the sounds he produces and of the possible meanings that may (or may not) be obtained from them by one enculturated to the same system. His choices are not limitless, however, for sets of relations are already bound into the system, that is, the system is itself structured and has social origins. Some structuralists refer to this kind of causality as *metonymic*. In metonymy, cause and effect are not related in the mousetrap manner of the Type I system. There are instead bundles and chains of possible effects which may either emerge or remain submerged within a structure.[2]

Before proceeding further, a theoretical problem can be seen to arise as a consequence of the formulation of the idea of a system of this kind. In any language, or in any semiological system, do the sets of constituitive elements constitute a denumerable set? That is, how "infinite'' a set is a language? May each element be counted? This is a problem of the kind posed by Cantor in the 1870s with respect to natural numbers.[3] Although no one has offered a solution, it seems worthwhile at this point to examine it tentatively for the illumination it sheds on the structuralist idea of a system.

From an empirical standpoint, we might proceed several ways, but perhaps the simplest way is to employ the same procedure we would in attempting to show that the set of rational numbers is denumerable. This involves taking each element and attempting to assign it a place on X, Y coordinates. We might attempt this with English as a system, opening the *Oxford English Dictionary* (which admittedly does not contain all the word elements of English but is a good place to start) and begin on page 1. We see at once that there are three and a half pages devoted to the element a. We must attempt to assign a place to each of the possible uses of a. It finds one use as the indefinite article; we accordingly assign it place x_1 in Figure 8.10. It is also used as an abbreviation, as in A.D.; this a can become x_2; the sailor's *aye* is understood by some not as *eye* but as *ay*, and this becomes x_3. There is its use in specifying time: we say "ten a-clock" not "ten oh-clock"; this becomes x_4. If we proceed this way, we should be able to enumerate separately all the linguistic signs in the *Oxford English Dictionary*; this would include all parts of words that serve as distinctive signs and all separate letters that do so.

The set of linguistic signs in English, taken at any one time in the language's history, appears likely to be a denumerable set. We have not proven this to be so, but it seems that we could proceed through

Figure 8.10
Denumeration Matrix

x_6 ...   .

x_3 x_5 ...   .

x_1 x_2 x_4 x_7 ... ...

the *Oxford English Dictionary* and perform the kind of operation we began with the letter *a*, assigning a separate place in *X*, *Y* for each element.

The question then arises: Is the set of possible relations *between* elements denumerable? This is a more profound question than the first. Since *meaning* is given by the relations among the elements and not by the elements themselves, such a set, if denumerable, would exceed many times the number of elements in the set. This is true not only because of the possible numbers of combinations and permutations of the finite number of now denumerated elements, which should approach ($N!$) or n factorial, but by the fact that the same pair of elements (for example) may signify more than one meaning. With respect to syntagmatic sequencing, of course, only certain sequences of elements remain permissible.

However, if the history of ideas tells us anything (and I believe that even Foucault would concede it does), it shows that new or different meanings are constantly being discovered within prior existing arrangements of elements. In the last chapter we saw how Durkheim, by the transformation *God = Society*, created an entire new discourse about an already extensive structuring of elements. This implies that some element (say, x_4) of Figure 8.10 can be used in place of some other element (say $x_8 9$) and an entire new discourse emerge from it. This is an integrated system of meanings and not simply one new element. The set of possible meanings, if indeed denumerable, must be excessively large.

This problem is central to the idea of a system of action of the Type III variety, which characterizes contemporary structuralist thought. Its mathematical solution could shed considerable light on the nature of systems of signs and the possible limits they impose on our ability to conceptualize and to articulate conceivable meanings.

The social sciences emerged within the academy as an attempt to explain society in terms of the Type I system. In this system the predominant features are elements or things in themselves (essences) and the causal connections linking them, all of which are assumed to have an existence independent of the observer but subject to adequate classification and identification by use of subjective categories. This was the claim not only of the St. Simonians but of the historicists as well. Despite the distinction Wilhelm Dilthey tried to establish between natural and social phenomena and which Weber sought to promulgate in his book of essays *The Methodology of the Social Sciences*,[4] the inherited procedures of *identification* and *classification* as constituting science appears to have restricted the social sciences in one way or another. *Classification* is the ordering of concepts into groups (or sets) on the basis of their relationships, by associations of contiguity, similarity, or both.[5] *Identification*, on the other hand, involves assigning an item to the group or set of the classification. Kenneth Bailey presents a schema for these operations, which is shown in Figure 8.11.

Figure 8.11 (a) shows classification (or conceptualization) alone, without identification and assignment to a set. This is what Robert Winch terms the heuristic, best exemplified by Weber's *ideal type*.[6] This creates a hypothetical, nonempirical type, extreme on all dimensions. Weber's ideal type of *economic man* is perfectly rational, perfectly self-interested, and concerned only with material interests.[7] Samples cannot be identified and placed within this category, for the category has been mentalistically constructed by intentionally exaggerating to the extreme all the characteristics defining the type. Figure 8.11(b) shows data analysis on the empirical level without benefit of prior conceptualization. This is the phenomenological and ethnographic approach typified by various forms of "participant observation," particularly those laying claim to a *tabula rasa* approach. It is also typified by cluster analysis and various other techniques employing frequency distributions as significant determinants. Observation occurs, common properties are determined, and classification into types occurs as a consequence. Winch refers to this as the empirical approach. Bailey refers to Figure 8.11(c) as the "classical" approach. Here an investigator

Figure 8.11

Bailey's Typology of Operations

Type ⟶	Heuristic	Empirical	Classical
Operations	(a)	(b)	(c)
Classification	X	Y	Z
Identification	$\downarrow$ none	$\uparrow$ Y,	$\downarrow$ Z,

constructs a type concept or an entire typology in his mind and then sets out to see how many specimens he can find (identify) to fit into the already constructed categories. This usually results in the four-cell contingency table. Bailey extends Winch's heuristic-empirical distinction here to include both conceptual and empirical operations within one framework and proceeds to show how both monothetic and polythetic typologies may be constructed from the classical type. Thus, the separate operations of induction and deduction of (a) and (b) are both employed in (c). Proceeding by both inductive and deductive reasoning in this way is consistent with Lévi-Strauss's structuralism, as we saw on p. 62. It is also consistent with the treatment given by Stinchcomb,[8] defended by Blalock,[9] Parsons,[10] and Lazarsfeld,[11] and forms the basis of Glazer and Strauss's "grounded theory."[12] It is not always necessary to hypothesize directions of relationships between variables nor to engage in statistical testing of hypotheses to make use of the procedure specified in (c). The hypothetico-deductive model is only one embodiment of the procedure shown in (c). It is most often employed in attempts to demonstrate a natural science form of causality between the conceptualized classes. Frequency of occurrence of one pair of classes is found to be greater or less than some other pair of classes, and this frequency is taken as indicative of some relation existing independently of the conceptualized classes themselves. However, since the frequencies are not in the classes but in the empirical things thus identified, the hypothetico-deductive model often fails, because of the need for establishing some external epistemic correlation between the classes and things. That is, since meanings do not exist in numbers and frequencies, such meanings must be applied to them by language, where they solely exist. Only if language can be mapped directly to things, only if words are signs for things in themselves and not simply signs for other signs of their own kind, can any epistemic correlation exist between concepts and things. This is true even on the assumptions of System I. From the standpoint of System III, hypothesis testing of the social-science variety is clearly a specious enterprise. Language is a self-contained system, arbitrary in its signification. A meaning is not a thing that may be pointed to and mapped in some coterminous way by statistical tests in terms of variables. At most, what such tests may show is something about the association between words, not between things. Our examples drawn from Osgood's semantic differential and from Romney and D'Andrade are efforts to do exactly that.

Within social science, all three versions of classification and identification shown in Figure 8.11 are employed. This has in part accounted for the diversity within these discourses. In the classical procedure (c), statistical testing has at last yielded its central position to correlation testing, returning to Durkheimian concomitant variation as the theoretical problems of inferring causal connections became more apparent. However, both multiple regression techniques and path analysis are limited to the mousetrap model of System I and to the problems raised by the need for epistemic correlation.

While the Type II system has proven invaluable in the natural sciences and technology, where systems are either intentionally designed or highly immutable, it has been less successful in the social sciences because of the problem raised by its nonrecursive metric. In physical, medical, or electronic systems, flow paths may be opened and measurements made under both open-loop and closed-loop conditions. Thus, the transfer functions of the functional elements may be measured and computed. In the social sciences this has proven to be impossible.[13] Such things as social systems, cultural systems, and personality systems, to the extent that they can be said to have ontological status, cannot be removed from the overall action system and studied *in insula*. Thus, transfer functions cannot be measured or computed, since causes may not be isolated from effects. Experimental procedures such as those employing small groups or the infamous laboratory experiments performed by otherwise well-meaning social psychologists always fail since they do not remove the individual from history, socialization, or education. Such subjects, however naive, are not truly isolated in the same sense that we can isolate an amplifier or gyroscope and determine its characteristics. Thus, although systems theory and cybernetic theory seemed to offer a great deal as presented to social science by George Klir,[14] Walter Buckley,[15] and Ludwig von Bertalanfy, it has proven difficult to employ in practice and has consequently served only as an overall organizational scheme for its champions. It too is subject to the same attack by structuralism as that presented to the Type I system. Although the causal claim is less pronounced in the Type II system than in the Type I system, the distinction between such concepts as *culture* and *society*, for example, is a difference existing only in language. Such a distinction is made only for the purposes of a particular discourse, and having been made, it binds one to other contingencies of the resulting structure of that discourse. The structural-functionalist model of stratification, for example, has no objective ontological status. Neither does such a thing as *socioeconomic status*. One does not perceive of himself as a *status inconsistent*. These are consequences of a particular way of ordering a discourse. A cynical structuralist may retort that socioeconomic status is an invention of social scientists to give themselves more status in the world than they actually have in the eyes of others. Since a true statistic based on constant variation, in Norbert Wiener's sense, is probably impossible to obtain for social phenomena, the cybernetic model will remain an elegant one for the social sciences, but one from which we can expect very little in terms of explanation or understanding. Econometrics shows that social phenomena are indeed nonrecursive in their nature, but it is unable to adequately treat these phenomena because of the metric problem.

It is partially as a response to the failures of the Type I and Type II systems that the Type III system has emerged. It dispenses with the hypothetico-deductive model. What is held to produce social effects is not some mysterious cause, some agency operating on its own property of inevitability, like a force in physics or an angel in medieval theology, but the internal structuring itself. This has proven to be a boon to Marxism, and Louis Althusser has been quick to seize on its possibilities. With cause and effect both immanent in structures rather than functional consequences of external agencies, Althusser's *metonymy* is a reassertion of Georg Simmel's forms of sociation, with their own internal contradictions. But unlike Simmel's forms, these structures are seen to lie midway between form and content, mediating both, with potential for moving in either direction. As we have seen, such an emergent potential comes about because the signifiers employed in discourse do not contain things in themselves, but only the potential for the articulation of things. Thus, although conventional social science, whether it employs the Type I system or the Type II system, must divide its operations into classification and identification, structuralism need not do this while remaining consistent with its Type III approach. Of course, it *may* do so. Certainly both Lévi-Strauss and Foucault do so, but this is not dictated by the nature of the system. For Althusser such operations are clearly obfuscating.

In a recent paper, Charles C. Lemert has argued that structuralism promises a solution to the problem of competing sociological methodologies.[16] According to Lemert, neither the formalists (Blalock, Parsons, Blau, Stinchcomb) nor the interpretavists (Cicourel, Garfinkle, Sacks, Bitner) have understood the nature of structure and particularly social structure. They accordingly talk past each other, most notably with their discussions of the relation between complex social structures and the contextual relativity that language imposes. Lemert proposes a sociology derived from Saussure in which measurement and identification are retained but recourse is made to a semantic encyclopedia of types of structures and types of articulations. He sees such an encyclopedia as encouraging replication. But replication has not characterized sociological discourse in the past because of the very diversity in discourses of a social science variety. By limiting such discourses to measurement and identification, he is attempting to constrain such discourses to the hypothetico-deductive model implicit in Figure 8.11(c), where the need for replication is at its highest. He is accordingly working against the liberating manifesto of Foucault and committing some of those sins which Foucault warns us against. But he is also working for the retention of the idea of a social science, discourse directed to an understanding of society. It may be necessary for the social scientist to be a sinner if he is to understand his world.

In American sociology, Lemert is one of a very few to have seriously considered the challenge that structuralism represents. In his book, *Sociology and the Twilight of Man: Homocentrism and Discourse in Sociological Theory*, Lemert takes up Foucault's "death of man" thesis and explores the homocentric bias of contemporary social theorists.[17] When he has concluded his analysis, he quotes Foucault:

From within language experienced and traversed as language, in the play of its possibilities extended to their furthest point, what emerges is that man has "come to an end," and that by reaching the summit of all possible speech, he arrives not at the very heart of himself but at the brink of that which limits him; in that region where death prowls, where thought is extinguished, where the promise of the origin interminably recedes.[18]

Lemert then goes on:

Though one cannot yet be sure, it is likely that this is the twilight region where a surprising nonpluralistic sociology now finds itself. If one were to guess what sociology might look like on the other side, it would be reasonable to imagine a relativistic, decentered manless world of talkers talking about talk and texts written about texts. If one finds this a morbidly cold place, one can ask two speculative questions. What evidence is there that when man makes himself the moral center that life is more human? What reason is there to believe that when sociology is done *homocentrically* it is able to account reliably for the increasingly marginal position of human creatures in a technologically and biologically precarious world?[19]

Lemert, in his book, does not attempt to point a new direction for sociological inquiry; it is in the later paper that the encyclopedia is suggested as a possibility. He is content to take up structuralist discourse as criticism, and he applies his criticism with devastating effect to much of what presently passes as contemporary social theory. Similarly, in attempting to explicate the idea of a system in structuralist thought, we found it necessary to refrain from suggesting what direction may be most promising or what principal criticisms a more traditional sociology may level against semiology and its institutional supports. With respect to the latter, it seems clear that such support is considerably weaker than the vast material apparatus marshalled by the various academic disciplines in possible defense of their respective turfs, which structuralism appears to challenge. And with regard to the former, we have attempted a measure of value neutrality in order to provide as clear an explication of this idea of a system as possible. Its implications for the generation of new sociological theory are not as clear at this point as its challenge to a traditionalist sociology. The sociologist is placed in the position of the accused before the impatient judge who asks, "Do you plead guilty or not guilty?" and can only reply, wonderingly, as the accused replied, "What else have you got?"

Perhaps this disquieting reply is necessary at this point in the development of social science, as a reminder that something "else," some other alternative, must be possible. Otherwise the death sentence may be imposed.

In the idea of a system articulated in structuralist discourse, reality, however this is understood, has become not simply one half of a Cartesian dichotomy, not simply the object member of the object-subject binary opposition and therefore external to the subject and estranged from him in a Kantian sense. Nor is there any form of object-subject unity such as that presupposed in certain phenomenologies. Such reality is also external to the system of signification employed by the observing subject and takes whatever status it attains only as he intentionally orders it by employing those sets of relations furnished him by his collectivity. What binds him in his discourse and what limits his perceptions of reality are the constraints, both internal and external, to the various socially endowed discourses about him, the regimes and programs already laid out before him as philosophies, rhetorics, science, and folklore. Words accordingly fail us as we attempt to predict, in mousetrap fashion, what is happening in the flight of Zeno's arrow or in the collision of Hume's famous balls. Within the discourses in which these possibilities are formulated there does not exist the language to treat them.

Michel Foucault believes he knows what these constraints are, and enumerates them for us. The abuses to which such self-constricting discourse may lead us have been discussed by him in a number of works, beginning with *Madness and Civilization*. It has remained for certain other investigators, who often employ structuralist approaches without admitting to it, to document critical areas Foucault has neglected. Christopher Lasch, for example, has unloosed a biting critique of the sins of American social science in his *Culture of Narcissism* and *Haven in a Heartless World*.[20] With respect to the Chicago school's arbitrary definition of a folk-urban dichotomy, Lasch reminds us that:

The Chicago School succeeded not so much in banishing history from sociological analysis as in banishing it as an object of explicit analysis. Its work depended at every point on a contrast between folk society and urban society, but it never stopped to examine the historical process through which one evolved from the other. That process remained implicit but unanalyzed. The antithesis between traditional society and urban society served merely as a typology; in the absence of historical analysis, the more that antithesis was elaborated, the more rigid, lifeless, obvious and banal it became. The worst thing that can be said of generalizations about the disintegrating impact of urban life is not that they seem unconvincing but, on the contrary, that they provoke almost automatic consent. This agreement suggests a paucity of content and a form that makes them impossible to refute. Once we accept the initial antithesis between folk and urban societies—between "traditional" and modern societies—we can hardly object to anything that derives from it. Sociologists might better have concerned themselves with analyzing the validity of the categories than with endlessly elaborating new versions of them.[21]

Although Lasch does not employ structuralist nomenclature, his method presupposes the variety of systems we have been examining. He goes on to show how these early assumptions excluded other more likely possibilities and how they have consequently resulted in a discourse about the family that, transmitted into popular culture, has aborted many of its functions. He is even less kind to the Parsonians in this matter.

Once social theory is viewed as a set of discourses, the social sciences are challenged in a manner quite apart from any criticism that scientistic orientations may take. We managed to analyze Weberian and Durkheimian formulations in the previous chapter on the basis of relatively few structuralist principles. Sociology here becomes a kind of game of acrostics, a play on words, a search for an appropriate phrase to cleverly encode some other words. While this may be a delightful diversion for those of us engaged in it, Lasch reminds us that it is a dangerous game that has already done extensive damage to quite innocent and unsuspecting people. The ordinary person mentioned in Chapter 1, the darling of ethnomethodologists and dramaturgical sociologists, has confirmed for him what he always suspected: grammarians and sociologists simply articulate, in an arcane language to which they alone have been educated, either common-sense axioms that have been communal property for generations or utter nonsense. What structuralism does is validate the ordinary person's view. If we take the most noteworthy formulations of the social sciences, this seems to be the case. Psychology has its frustration-aggression principle, anthropology its incest taboo, economics its supply-demand curves, and sociology its latent functions. These stand out by the degree of certainty we ascribe to them, and they constitute social science as *science* with a wealth of empirical evidence to support them. It takes little reflection, however, to concede that these are only the most trivial expressions, couched in the nomenclatures of particular discourses, of folk wisdoms we have always had. A child learns in the playground that if a playmate does not "get his way," he will become hostile. That one should buy cheap and sell dear was certainly known to Pharaoh's keeper of the granaries, and that often "things get out of hand" but somehow manage to "work themselves out" despite us, which is what latent functions are all about, finds expression in innumerable adages and saws of traditional cultures. The universality of prohibitions on incest is taken for granted by the political "man on the street," independently of what anthropologists say. The distinction between traditional and urban society devolves to a way of speaking, and none of these utterances seems as profound as, for example, the laws governing the swing of a simple pendulum or the fact that a friend will go to considerable expense and effort to assure that our birthday will be a happy occasion. This is not to demean the social sciences or to belittle the aspirations of its founders or our best colleagues. But with the possibilities opened for us by a system of the Type III variety, it does begin to appear that we may have been asking the wrong questions. If something like a science of society is indeed possible, then it is unlikely that we shall be able to securely found it by recourse to the mousetrap or kite analogies. The Type III system is probably not the answer either, but it does point to the problem confronting us. Semiology is unlikely to be the destiny of the social sciences; like French symbolism or French existentialism, however, its specter will continue to haunt us long after its demise as another intellectual movement.

A philosophy of social science can do little to bolster the findings of a discourse that ignores the fact that prior to all other claims it is first and foremost a discourse. It must reexamine its premises, consider paths not taken, and constantly guard against the kinds of errors its grammar may demand of it. Since I am allowing myself a measure of personal license at this point, I freely admit that it is time to question whether or not we wish to continue to defend ourselves in the name of science. Some of us are content to acknowledge that what we are engaged in is a discourse that treats of man as a social being and the ways in which he appears to organize his world. That, it seems to me, is a sufficiently grand and noble enterprise to merit one's serious attention. We can now leave to computers the gross task of accumulating and processing data of a wholly empirical kind, using them as examples of what we are talking about, not as proofs of scientific claims. And we can begin to discuss why it is that such words as ''grand'' and ''noble'' in the sense that they have been used here have been excluded by the social sciences in their attempts to study man as a social being, and whether perhaps we have not made some mistake there in the ordering of our discourse.

Notes

1. Claude E. Shannon and Warren Weaver, *The Mathematical Theory of Communication* (Urbana: University of Illinois Press, 1949).

2. M. Glucksmann, *Structuralist Analysis in Contemporary Social Thought* (Boston: Routledge and Kegan Paul, 1974), p. 148.

· 3. For a discussion of Cantor's theorem and the problem of denumerability of sets, see Sherman K. Stein, *Mathematics, the Man-made Universe* (San Francisco: Freeman, 1963), esp. pp. 252ff.

4. New York: Free Press, 1949.

5. Kenneth Bailey, "Monothetic and Polythetic Typologies and Their Relation to Conceptualization, Measurement, and Scaling," *American Sociological Review* 38(1), 1973, p. 19.

6. Robert F. Winch, "Heuristic and Empirical Typologies: A Job for Factor Analysis," *American Sociological Review* 12(1), 1947.

7. Bailey, 1973, pp. 19ff.

8. Arthur L. Stinchcomb, *Constructing Social Theories* (New York: Harcourt, 1968), p. 32.

9. Hubert M. Blalock, Jr., *Theory Construction: From Verbal to Mathematical Formulations* (Englewood Cliffs, N.J.: Prentice-Hall, 1969).

10. Talcott Parsons, *The Structure of Social Action* (Glencoe, Ill.: Free Press, 1937), pp. 601–24.

11. Paul F. Lazarsfeld, "Some Remarks on the Typological Procedures in Social Research," *Zeitschrift fur Sozialforschuung* 6, pp. 119–39.

12. Barney G. Glazer and Anselm L. Strauss, *The Discovery of Grounded Theory* (Chicago: Aldine, 1967).

13. Hubert M. Blalock, Jr., *Social Statistics* 2d ed. (New York: McGraw-Hill, 1972) advises that "whenever there is thought to be reciprocal causation of feedback from the 'dependent' variable to any of the others, simultaneous equations must be used" (p. 431) and cites Carl Christ's *Econometric Models and Methods* (New York: Wiley, 1966) and J. Johnston's *Econometric Methods* (New York: McGraw-Hill, 1963). Since it deals with intervally scaled variables, econometrics is clearly in the best position to explore the possibility of nonrecursive measurements. However, it is also clear that econometrics has had little success in this direction. Johnston (1963), whom Blalock (1972) cites, warns that only in recursive models will ordinary least squares provide an estimating technique and that in the more general simultaneous equation model, where assumptions of the recursive model are not fulfilled, the method of indirect least squares may be used. This involves a great deal of estimation of the possible value of metrics, however, "and the derived structural estimators are likely to be biased" (pp. 376ff). Wiener was right, of course. The kinds of statistical measures employed to sell a program on the basis of scientism in sociology can lay no claim to reality. It is significant that as the world economy falters badly, increased numbers of economists are employed by government to rationalize the failures of the system but can do little to improve it.

14. George Klir, *An Approach to General Systems Theory* (New York: Van Nostrand, 1969).

15. Walter Buckley, *Sociology and Modern Systems Theory* (Englewood Cliffs, N.J.: Prentice-Hall, 1967).

16. Charles C. Lemert, ''Language, Structure, and Measurement: Structuralist Semiotics and Sociology,'' *American Journal of Sociology* 84(4), 1979.

17. Charles C. Lemert, *Sociology and the Twilight of Man: Homocentrism and Discourse in Sociological Theory* (Carbondale: Southern Illinois University Press, 1979).

18. Lemert, 1979, p. 230, quoting Michel Foucault, *The Order of Things* (N.Y.: Vintage, 1973), p. 383.

19. Lemert, 1979, pp. 230–31.

20. Christopher Lasch, *The Culture of Narcissism* (New York: Norton, 1979); *Haven in a Heartless World* (New York: Basic Books, 1977).

21. Lasch, 1977, p. 35.

Selected Bibliography

Abrahamson, Mark. 1978. *Functionalism*. Englewood Cliffs, N.J.: Prentice-Hall.

Adorno, Theodor, ed. 1976. *The Positivist Dispute in German Sociology*. New York: Harper & Row.

Althusser, Louis. 1969. *For Marx*. London: Allen.

Badcock, C. R. 1975. "The Ecumenical Anthropologist: Solutions to Some Persistent Problems in Theoretical Sociology Found in the Works of Claude Lévi-Strauss." *British Journal of Sociology* 26(2).

Bailey, Kenneth. 1973. "Monothetic and Polythetic Typologies and Their Relation to Conceptualization, Measurement, and Scaling," *American Sociological Review* 38(1).

Bales, Robert F. 1950. *Interaction Process Analysis*. Cambridge, Mass.: Addison-Wesley.

———. 1970. *Personality and Interpersonal Behavior*. New York: Holt, Rinehart & Winston.

Barnes, Barry. 1974. *Scientific Knowledge and Sociological Theory*. London: Routledge & Kegan Paul.

Barthes, Roland. 1968. *Writing, Degree Zero, and Elements of Semiology*. Boston: Beacon Press.

———. 1972. *Mythologies*. New York: Hill & Wang.

———. 1975. *The Pleasures of the Text*. New York: Hill & Wang.

Bauman, Zygmunt. 1973. "The Structuralist Promise." *British Journal of Sociology* 24(1).

Bernstein, B. 1972. "Social Class, Language, and Socialization," in *Language and Social Context*, edited by Pier Paolo Giglioli. Middlesex: Penguin.

Blalock, Hubert M., Jr. 1969. *Theory Construction: From Verbal to Mathematical Formulations*. Englewood Cliffs, N.J.: Prentice-Hall.

————. 1969a. *Causal Inference in Nonexperimental Research*. Chapel Hill: University of North Carolina Press.

Brown, Roger. 1967. *Social Psychology*. New York: Free Press.

————. 1968. *Words and Things*. New York: Free Press.

Buckley, Walter. 1967. *Sociology and Modern Systems Theory*. Englewood Cliffs, N.J.: Prentice-Hall.

Cam, Helen. 1950. *England Before Elizabeth*. London: Hutchinson.

Christ, Carl. 1966. *Econometric Models and Methods*. New York: Wiley.

Clarke, Simon. 1978. "The Origins of Lévi-Strauss's Structuralism." *Sociology* 12(3).

Cohen, Jere. 1980. "Rational Capitalism in Renaissance Italy." *American Journal of Sociology* 84(6).

Cohen, Norman. 1970. *The Pursuit of the Millennium*. New York: Oxford University Press.

Culler, Jonathan. 1975. *Structuralist Poetics*. Ithaca, N.Y.: Cornell University Press.

————. 1976. *Ferdinand de Saussure*. Baltimore: Penguin.

Derrida, Jacques. 1976. *Of Grammatology*. Baltimore: Johns Hopkins University Press.

Durkheim, Émile. 1915. *The Elementary Forms of the Religious Life*. New York: Free Press.

————. 1951. *Suicide*. New York: Free Press.

Durkheim, Émile, and Marcel Mauss. 1963. *Primitive Classification*. Chicago: University of Chicago Press.

Eco, Umberto. 1976. *A Theory of Semiotics*. Bloomington: Indiana University Press.

Ehrmann, Jacques. 1966. *Structuralism*. Garden City, N.Y.: Doubleday.

Fauconnet, Paul. 1928. *La Responsibilité*. Paris: Alcan.

Foucault, Michel. 1976. *The Archaeology of Knowledge*. New York: Harper & Row.

————. 1980. *Power/Knowledge*. New York: Pantheon.

Glazer, Barney G., and Anselm Strauss. 1967. *The Discovery of Grounded Theory*. Chicago: Aldine.

Goldmann, Lucien. 1980. *Essays on Method in the Sociology of Literature*. St. Louis: Telos Press.

Gordon, Colin. 1980. "Bibliography: Writings of Michel Foucault." in M. Foucault, 1980.

Hawkins, Terrence. 1977. *Structuralism and Semiotics*. Berkeley: University of California Press.

Johnson, J. 1963. *Econometric Methods*. New York: McGraw-Hill.

Katz, Robert. 1964. *An Introduction to the Special Theory of Relativity*. New York: Van Nostrand.

Klir, George. 1969. *An Approach to General Systems Theory*. New York: Van Nostrand.

Kurzweil, Edith. 1977. "Ending the Era of Man." *Theory and Society* 4(3).

————. 1980. *The Age of Structuralism*. New York: Columbia University Press.

Laing, R. D., H. Phillipson, and A. R. Lee. 1966. *Interpersonal Perception*. New York: Harper & Row.

Lasch, Christopher. 1977. *Haven in a Heartless World*. New York: Harper & Row.

————. 1979. *The Culture of Narcissism*. New York: Norton.

Lawrence, Peter. 1976. *Georg Simmel, Sociologist and European*. New York: Barnes & Noble.

Lemert, Charles. 1979. *Sociology and the Twilight of Man*. Carbondale: University of Southern Illinois Press.

————. 1979a. "Language, Structure, and Measurement: Structuralist Semiotics and Sociology." *American Journal of Sociology* 84(4).

Lemert, Charles, and Willard A. Nielsen. 1982. "Structures, Instruments, and Reading in Sociology." In *Structural Sociology*, edited by Ino Rossi. New York: Columbia University Press.

Levine, Donald. 1976. "Simmel's Influence on American Sociology." *American Journal of Sociology* 81(3 and 4).

Lévi-Strauss, Claude. 1963. *Structural Anthropology*. New York: Basic Books.

————. 1963a. *The Scope of Anthropology*. London: Cape.

Lukács, Georg. 1971. *The Theory of the Novel*. Cambridge, Mass.: MIT Press.

Mannheim, Karl. 1968. *Essays on the Sociology of Knowledge*. London: Routledge & Kegan Paul.

Merton, Robert K. 1957. *Social Theory and Social Structure*. New York: Free Press.

Miller, Delbert C. 1977. *Handbook of Research Design and Social Measurement*. 3d ed. New York: David McKay.

Mizruchi, Ephraim H. 1983. *Regulating Society: Marginality and Social Control in Historical Perspective*. New York: Free Press.

Morris, Charles. 1946. *Signs, Language, and Behavior*. New York: Braziller.

Nelson, Benjamin. 1973. "Weber's 'Protestant Ethic': Its Origins, Wanderings, and Foreseeable Futures." In *Beyond the Classics?*, edited by Charles Y. Glock and Phillip E. Hammond. New York: Harper & Row.

————. 1974. "Max Weber's 'Author's Introduction' (1920): A Master Clue to His Main Aims." *Sociological Inquiry* 44(1).

Ogden, C. K., and I. A. Richards. 1923. *The Meaning of Meaning*. New York: Harcourt Brace.

Osgood, Charles E., George Suci, and P. H. Tannenbaum. 1958. *The Measurement of Meaning.* Urbana: University of Illinois Press.

Parsons, Talcott. 1937. *The Structure of Social Action.* Glencoe, Illinois: Free Press.

———. 1951. *The Social System.* New York: Free Press.

———. 1961. "An Outline of the Social System." In Parsons et al., *Theories of Society,* vol. 1. New York: Free Press.

Parsons, Talcott, and R. F. Bales. 1955. *Family, Socialization, and Interaction Process.* New York: Free Press.

Parsons, Talcott, R. F. Bales, and Edward Shils. 1953. *Working Papers in the Theory of Action.* New York: Free Press.

Parsons, Talcott, and E. Shils. 1951. *Toward a General Theory of Action.* New York: Harper & Row.

Pettit, Philip. 1977. *The Concept of Structuralism.* Berkeley: University of California Press.

Phillips, D. C. 1972. "The Methodological Basis of Systems Theory." *Academy of Management Journal* 15(4).

———. 1976. *Holistic Thought in Social Science.* Stanford, Calif.: Stanford University Press.

Piaget, Jean. 1968. *Structuralism.* New York: Harper & Row.

Romney, A. K., and R. D'Andrade. 1964. "Cognitive Aspects of English Kin Terms." *American Anthropologist* 66(3).

Rossi, Ino, ed. 1982. *Structural Sociology.* New York: Columbia University Press.

———. 1982a. *The Logic of Culture: Advances in Structural Theory and Methods.* South Hadley, Mass.: J. F. Bergin.

Routh, Jane, and Janet Wolff, eds. 1977. *The Sociology of Literature: Theoretical Approaches.* Keeler Staffordshire: University of Keel.

Sapir, Edward. 1921. *Language.* New York: Harcourt Brace.

Saussure, Ferdinand de. 1966. *Course in General Linguistics.* New York: McGraw-Hill.

Shannon, Claude E., and Warren Weaver. 1949. *The Mathematical Theory of Communication.* Urbana: University of Illinois Press.

Simmel, Georg. 1971. *On Individuality and Social Forms.* Chicago: University of Chicago Press.

Smart, J. J. C. 1963. *Philosophy and Scientific Realism.* New York: Humanities Press.

Spykman, Nicholas J. 1966. *The Social Theory of Georg Simmel.* New York: Atherton.

Stanley, Manfred. 1979. *The Technological Conscience.* New York: Free Press.

Stein, Sherman K. 1963. *Mathematics, the Man-made Universe.* San Francisco: Freeman.

Stinchcomb, Arthur L. 1968. *Constructing Social Theories*. New York: Harcourt.

Trevelyan, G. M. 1925. *England in the Age of Wycliff*. London: Longmans.

Von Bertalanfy, Ludwig. 1972. "The History and Status of General Systems Theory." *Academy of Management Journal* 15(4).

Wallimann, Isidor, H. Rosenbaum, N. Tatsis, and G. V. Zito. 1980. "Misreading Weber: The Concept of Macht." *Sociology* (U.K.)

Weber, Max. 1958. *The Protestant Ethic and the Spirit of Capitalism*. New York: Scribner's.

Whorf, Benjamin Lee. 1956. *Language, Thought, and Reality*. Cambridge, Mass.: MIT Press.

Wiener, Norbert. 1948. *Cybernetics*. New York: Wiley.

Wilson, Edmund. 1931. *Axel's Castle: A Study of the Imaginative Literature of 1870–1930*. New York: Scribner's.

Winch, Peter. 1958. *The Idea of a Social Science and Its Relation to Philosophy*. London: Routledge & Kegan Paul.

Winch, Robert F. 1947. "Heuristic and Empirical Typologies: A Job for Factor Analysis." *American Sociological Review* 12(1).

Zimmerman, Jacquelyne. 1979. "Similarities Between Hugo and Lukács." Unpublished. Ithaca, N.Y.: Cornell University.

Zito, George V. 1973. "Durkheimian Suicides in Shakespeare." *Omega* 4(4).

———. 1975. *Methodology and Meanings: The Varieties of Sociological Inquiry*. New York: Holt, Rinehart & Winston.

———. 1975a. *Sociological Concepts*. Columbus, Ohio: Charles Merrill.

———. 1977. "Giovanni's Ladder: Early Franciscan and Social Scientific Thought." Paper given at the annual meeting of the Eastern Sociological Society, New York.

———. 1979. "Attribution and Symbolic Interaction: An Impasse at the Generalized Other." *Human Relations* 32(7).

———. 1983. "Toward a Sociology of Heresy." *Sociological Analysis* 44(2).

———. 1984. "Agamemnon and Oedipus: The New American Culture." Paper given at the annual meeting of the American Culture Association, Toronto.

Index

156   Index

About the Author

GEORGE V. ZITO is Associate Professor of Sociology at Syracuse University. His previously published works include *Methodology and Meanings, Sociological Concepts, Population and Its Problems*, and *Civilization and Society*.